—THE—
BALANCED
HORSE

—THE—
BALANCED
HORSE

The Aids by Feel, Not Force

SYLVIA LOCH

TRAFALGAR SQUARE
North Pomfret, Vermont

First published in the United States of America in 2013 by
Trafalgar Square Books
North Pomfret, Vermont 05053

ISBN 978-1-57076-622-0
Library of Congress Control Number: 2012955689

Designed and typeset by Paul Saunders
Printed in China

The Balanced Horse is dedicated to all my friends in Portugal
and in particular to the Breeders of the noble Lusitano horse,
who has helped me to understand all horses.
With profound gratitude.

SYLVIA LOCH

CONTENTS

'How can we obtain this tact, this keenness of perception, this refined and rapid feeling of all the efforts of the horse in every degree, preparing the efforts which are going to follow? This cannot be taught in a book. For these faculties we require, practice, work, and, above all things, natural aptitude and love for horses.'

JAMES FILLIS, *Breaking and Riding 1902*

FOREWORD

By Carl Hester MBE

Dressage is quite simply about training and to be able to train a horse the rider needs to be able to communicate to the horse in a clear way – no mixed signals! Whilst I am training my horses and riders as athletes for competition, I believe that every horse and every rider will get more out of their relationship if the rider understands and works to make his or her signals to the horse as clear as possible.

I have known of Sylvia's work over several years and from time to time we've met at various equestrian events – the Spanish Riding School of Vienna involvement being something we both share in common. Sylvia's books are widely read throughout the dressage world and it is a pleasure to be asked to write about *The Balanced Horse*.

What riders need to understand about the aids – the signals – is the subtleties and Sylvia explains the feel, position and timing in a user-friendly way that will help any rider at any level.

When I started my dressage career I was very lucky to ride some advanced schoolmaster horses which took some of the trial and error out of the equation. Unfortunately, not everyone gets that sort of opportunity – so a book like this will be invaluable to all those who are seeking to get it right from the start, and develop their own awareness of how their aids influence the horse.

Even at Grand Prix level, riders can still make mistakes and even the best horse in the world can only do what the rider has told him. Now, with the help of Sylvia's book, riders of all levels can build up a real mental picture in their head of what they should or should not be doing for each and every movement. I believe this to be one of the most important aspects of dressage as the horse can read us like a book, but once we have got it right in our head, he will follow. The quotes at the end of each chapter from riders and trainers from previous centuries to present day make a fascinating and inspiring addition – a proof that correct communication will work with any horse, whatever his breed, colour or size.

Best wishes

CARL

WHY I WROTE THIS BOOK

HAVING PRONOUNCED, a few years back, that I did not feel motivated to write another book on schooling and dressage – since I felt I had said it all – I surprised myself by accepting a request for another book by my commissioning editor John Beaton of Kenilworth. If truth be known, it was the photographs that inspired me.

In May, 2011, great friends of ours, Henry and Eugenie Askew, reopened their stunning nineteenth-century indoor riding school at the family home, Ladykirk in Berwickshire. Their new tenant was Lucy Simpson, who had come to me for dressage lessons. As a qualified Monty Roberts instructor, she was looking for somewhere in the Borders to start up a training yard, so I had introduced her to the Askew family.

Years of painstaking research, careful planning and love had gone into the restoration of Ladykirk's classical buildings. To celebrate the transformation of the indoor school, Henry generously gave me permission to hold my annual BHS Borders Festival of the Horse demonstration within its lofty portals.

'Dressage in Lightness' was to bring in literally hundreds of people and I know quite well that it was certainly as much to do with seeing Ladykirk as it was to seeing me riding and teaching! By this time, Lucy was installed and the beautiful stables were brimming with horses. Present at the event were a number of photographers, including some good friends, and it is from their work that the first seeds for another book were sown.

We have had thousands of photos taken over the years, mainly for magazine articles, yet nothing prepared me for the sheer drama of these pictures.

My once dappled grey Lusitano stallion, now aged 16, and white as snow, etches himself on those austere white walls with energy and poise. Prazer first came to my yard, unbalanced, stumbling and knowing nothing of dressage; now – all those years of training, his patient endeavour – seem cemented in each image. A special afternoon, a great audience, a fantastic backdrop – quite clearly the nobility of the horse, the proof of what dressage means to me – had to be shared.

The idea of a purely photographic book was discussed. I sent John the photos and the response was immediate: he and Kenilworth Press wanted go ahead. At the time, I was experiencing severe illness within the family and a lot of difficulties at home so I knew hours of writing would be impossible. How about a book on the aids, I suggested, with just captions? That, I could just about manage. The response was not exactly what I had in mind, 'But without

Ladykirk Stableyard, built in 1840 and designed by Mr Tattersall of Pall Mall (*photograph by Stefan Lubomirski de Vaux*).

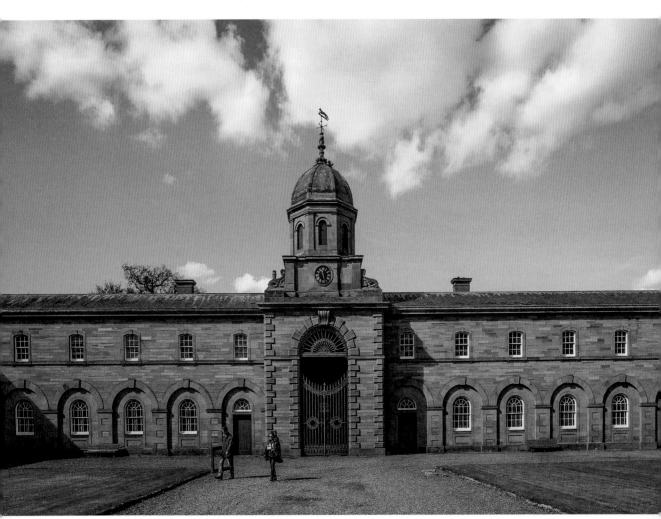

prose to accompany those magnificent pictures, Sylvia...' The sentence did not need completing.

A synopsis was sent and accepted. I began writing. How does one explain when a book takes on a life of its own? During this time of worry and heartache, I found the will and the inspiration to write properly. My daughter has always been one hundred per cent behind me with all my work, and I am very lucky to have some wonderful friends, but where and how was I going to find the time?

I can only say that, from somewhere deep down, I found the strength and the inspiration to make time. Sometimes, you just have to shut yourself away and commit. *The Balanced Horse* is the result; I could not resist it. Suddenly, there was so much to share, so much to show, I can only describe it like a flood. Far from writing captions, the prose just came flowing and flowing; my greatest difficulty was not writing too much!

As a Christian, I have always believed anything artistic or creative is a gift from God. I also believe that one's horses are heaven-sent, since each one I have taken on to train and school – and particularly Prazer, the stallion featured in this book – came unexpectedly. Yet, Prazer (which means pleasure in Portuguese) has been good enough to let me teach with him as well as train him to the highest levels. He accepts everything with verve and generosity. And that is the way that always seems to work. Few of my horses have ever been for me alone – except when I was competing – they all love the teaching.

There is no doubt that helping others to understand how the horse moves, and how he should feel, deepens and broadens our own theory of riding. Practising each exercise for oneself is wonderful; having the ability to teach that to another person on your most cherished horse, is awesome! Perception, self-examination and developing an eye for every little move in every little moment can be challenging, but it leads to greater scholarship and understanding.

Developing your student's sense of feel, by opening doors for them and doing so in partnership with a kind and generous horse takes you, the trainer, to new heights. Best of all, is the knowledge that you are not just helping your student, but other horses; all horses with whom they will come into contact for the rest of their lives. Prazer gives so much of himself in every lesson that I often wonder if he innately believes that too.

It may sound dramatic to say that the art and discipline of classical riding is such a profoundly good one – it changes your life. Of course, all riding should and can be classical but that is not always the case. You cannot work to any level without study, which is why I have always felt a common bond with those ideals first laid down by the Greeks and later in the writings of the great classical Masters from the post-Renaissance period right up to the modern day. From my understanding of their work, I am convinced they, too, drew drive and inspiration from outside themselves.

There is a balance in riding that can only come from adhering to Nature's laws. Schooling a horse without force all depends on principles which have nothing to do with man-made rules. Instead, one is drawing from a force that finds its origin in the Universe itself. For me, writing about the aids has been illuminating because I needed to put into simple language what I have learned over decades. I have been fortunate to know, watch and work with some of

Interior of the riding school (*photograph by Stefan Lubomirski de Vaux*).

the modern-day Masters. Today most have gone, which is why it is doubly important to demonstrate a way of riding that is in danger of being lost.

Further to this mention of the Masters, at the end of each chapter in this book you will find a list of 'classical quotes' – ideas about the subject matter of the chapter as expressed by some of the great riders, trainers and equestrian thinkers, both from times past and of the present. I hope these will serve both to inform and inspire you. Also, at the end of the book you will find a number of schooling exercises, listed chapter by chapter, which again relate to the subject matter discussed in each. I hope these will prove useful adjuncts to your own schooling regime.

ACKNOWLEDGEMENTS

Now for some personal tributes. Stefan Lubomirski de Vaux's generosity in allowing me those dramatic long shots of Ladykirk are greatly appreciated. A special thank-you must also go to Nathalie Todd whose eye for equine locomotion is second to none! Her stunning outdoor pictures of Queijada would simply not have been possible without the co-operation of Tina Elliot-Layton who has represented Great Britain internationally and who currently has the ride of my daughter's lovely Lusitano at Contessa in Hertfordshire.

John Beaton has been a very patient and skilful editor with whom to work, as has Martin Diggle with whom I've had the privilege to work before. Designer Paul Saunders has been quite extraordinary with his eye for balance and understanding of how I wanted the horses presented in this book. It is lovely when people really believe in what you are doing and have the vision to make it possible.

It has been such an honour to receive Carl's Foreword. He is such a talented rider and cares so much for his horses and the art of equitation, I can think of no better person to inspire future generations.

Where would I be without Angela Hinnigan, our Classical Riding Club administrator and again, my supportive daughter, Allegra? Both totally understand my lack of computer skills and have patiently helped with photos and files and generally held my hand throughout the technical compilation of this book.

Also a big thank-you to my understanding husband Richard, and to all my students for their enthusiasm and encouragement. Feedback from Lisa and Paul Scaglione from Oregon and Stephanie Plaster from Lancashire was especially helpful; Johanna Macarthur too. But most of all, I have to thank my horses – because without them I simply can't imagine what my life would be.

HORSES AND RIDERS

Since the majority of the photographs shown in this book were taken at a public demonstration for the BHS Borders Festival of the Horse at Ladykirk, in May 2011 and 2012, they were clearly not stage-managed. I have always believed in showing the work in progress. As regards the outdoor photos, these were taken during a one-hour flying visit to Contessa Stud, Hertfordshire where my daughter's horse Queijada has been on loan for the past four years and where we briefly got to know each other again as the camera whirred. The 'guest horses' who appear in some photos were turned out by their owners and I am grateful for the efforts they made. Regarding my own horse, Prazer, thank you to Judith Bellamy for turning him out so nicely. I presented him for both demonstrations in a double bridle but he is also ridden in a snaffle at home. I am deeply grateful to all owners, horses and riders alike for contributing towards *The Balanced Horse*. In approximate order of appearance, they are:

Prazer Lusitano stallion, 16 hh. aged 15, owned and ridden by the author

Queijada (known as 'Q') Lusitano mare, 16.2 hh. aged 14, owned by Allegra Loch and ridden here by the author

Bingh Dutch Warmblood gelding, 16.1 hh. aged 5, owned by Dalriada Sport Horses and ridden by Lucy Simpson

Colkitto (Abu) Dutch Warmblood stallion, 17 hh. aged 4, owned by Dalraida Sport Horses and ridden by Lucy Simpson

Porridge Coloured Cob gelding, 15.1 hh. aged 15, owned and ridden by Amanda Brumwell

INTRODUCTION

The object of Dressage is the harmonious development of the physique and ability of the horse. As a result it makes the horse calm, supple, loose and flexible, but also confident, attentive and keen, thus achieving perfect understanding with his rider.

FEI Rules

PERFECT UNDERSTANDING! How poignant are these words, and how often people express the wish for greater understanding in their relationships. Whether it's a partner, husband, wife or friends – too often we feel misunderstood and wish we could redress the balance.

Well, at least we can with our horses. This book is concerned, more than anything else, with developing that 'perfect understanding' which is so important in our riding relationships. You do not have to be a dressage rider to do this, although it is generally recognised that the techniques of dressage are appropriate for all our work with horses. Therefore, whether you hack, event, show, enjoy long distance riding, natural horsemanship or Western, the improvement of your horse through an understanding of 'his' language, should allow him greater ability, confidence and enjoyment in all your work together.

Since the horse cannot speak, and while commands may be given instantaneously and in a very rapid sequence, it is important to develop a language. Once we recognise this and use it correctly and fluently, confusion, misunderstanding and second guessing will become a thing of the past.

OPPOSITE In this book, each and every aid is examined separately and in minute detail. Nevertheless, it is the combined effect of all the aids, seen and unseen, which produces a good result. These must be supplied succinctly, with the release being as important as the application.

The Language of the Aids is not as well understood today as it should be. At one time it was the preserve of the schools of equitation, especially the cavalry schools, and was passed on to the general riding public through instructors well versed in the system. Generally, this language, based on certain laws and principles of Nature, was the same throughout the civilised world. So whether you rode in Vienna, Saumur, Lisbon, Madrid, Belgrade, Hanover, Stockholm, Milan, Oslo or Prague – you might not recognise the word spoken by your human companions, but the horses would understand you! This was true whatever the breed, whatever the occasion. The only differences would be ones of emphasis.

Today, we live in a very different world. With the demise of cavalry, traditional principles have disappeared and riding has gone through many changes – not always for the better. Contradictory advice is everywhere. Different countries now promote different styles, while teachers of little experience or understanding of the entire spectrum abound. Anyone, it seems, can teach. With the emphasis not so much about *how* to ride, but rather than *what* you ride, the aids are often forgotten. Everyone wants a good-looking horse and fashions for a 'certain type' come and go, as more and more treat riding as a social affair with success at competition high on the wish-list even of people of relatively little experience.

There is a greater turnover of horses too. Animals change hands if they are not seen to win, and insufficient riders have the patience, knowledge or finesse to school a young horse correctly from scratch. It should be a crime for an inexperienced rider to acquire an inexperienced horse, but how many are wise enough to know this? Those horses who develop 'issues' are often blamed for their behaviour, when actually it is the rider's job to prevent these happening in the first place. Generally, things go wrong when too much is expected too soon.

Along the way, it seems that the special Language of the Aids is frequently forgotten or fragmented, and I see this as the greatest tragedy in riding today. It will be the horse who suffers most when this happens. Often a highly talented animal will leave one country to move on to a new home elsewhere. The original trainer may well be one of the old school – who has presented the horse in the best light possible – but problems begin if the new owner is not versed in the Language of the Aids. The downside for the horse is not just the long journey, a new routine and environment; sadly, all he has learned in his previous school is no longer the *status quo*. Confusion and stress may lead to unwanted behaviour and, if the new owner is not patient or able to improve their own ability, the horse may become dangerous.

Whilst correct aiding can liberate the horse, incorrect aiding can exert a very adverse effect. For example, a strong clamp of the calf on a higher-level horse may cause him to run backward, offer a levade – more likely a rear – or stop him stone dead. And yet the trainer had said 'more leg!' – but not *how* or *where*. Pity no one had read the book …

For this reason it is hoped the pictures and annotations presented in this book will confirm in people's minds that there is a right and a wrong way of doing things. I have tried to highlight the fact that the Language of the Aids is as relevant today as it was in the past. Not everyone has time to read these days, but pictures can say more than a thousand words. Although the main body of this book shows my own horses working up the different levels, we have purposely also demonstrated with horses who have never had a dressage lesson in their lives before. The point has been to show that every horse will respond when simple classical principles are put into place.

As with the human body, the horse's body harbours many reactive pressure points. The power of touch is much underestimated and, in their natural habitat, we can see time after time, how horses respond to the tiniest stimuli. Over time and in the correct balance, we reach a point where each aid correctly applied can elicit a response as instant as the knee jerk reaction in our own. Since the classical aids are based on Nature's laws of equilibrium and gravity, each movement, each request can bring about a biomechanical effect. In this way, we can educate the horse to the point where, over time, many different patterns of behaviour will become automatic.

Muscle memory is a wonderful thing, but psychology plays a large part too. More than any other animal (perhaps with the exception of elephants), horses remember. Good and bad sensations are quickly assimilated so, provided each new request is coupled with good sensations and plenty of praise (positive reinforcement) the horse will generally want to return to that movement again and again.

In this way, we build up an established pattern of behaviour together, step by patient step. For the rider, this is very empowering, particularly since no force has had to be applied – rather the contrary. Generally, it is the cessation of the aid that invokes the best results. We ask – and the horse replies.

It is a happy day, when that special shared language can be developed from the simplest of requests to a polite dialogue. Developed by master horsemen over many centuries to complement the horse in all his movements, we have certainly inherited a marvellous legacy and it is there to be used.

I was lucky enough to be born at a time when there were still some great Masters of Equitation with whom to talk, study and thus be inspired. I know I

learned the most by watching – with certain special moments burned into my subconscious. My earnest wish in writing this book is that, by sharing these insights and how I have taken them forward in my own personal scholarship, this will in turn inspire and help others.

Classical equitation was never about dusty books on shelves, fuddy-duddy precepts or impossible ideals. It is about riding for real and, more than anything, about riding out into the light and opening doors! By processing all I have learned and presenting it into an accessible form for today's horse and today's rider, I hope I will help your riding to resonate with joy. At the end of the day it has to be about the horses themselves, and it was certainly they who have given me the courage to write this.

There is nothing better than riding a happy, balanced horse who glories in his sense of achievement. It somehow makes everything so right.

OPPOSITE As I address the audience, Prazer shows that he is very much part of the dialogue too.

BALANCE

Questions and Answers

Everyone talks wistfully about a balanced horse, but how many acknowledge that there are several balances?

There is the balance of the young horse, newly backed and not very strong behind. There is the balance of the old stager, who has happily carried children and their parents for years. There is the balance of the racehorse, hunter or jumper and there is all the difference in the world between the balance of the young dressage horse and that of the High School horse. Each can be perfect for his particular purpose; each may be woefully imperfect.

The latter is generally all to do with the rider. What a responsibility!

This begs a stream of questions. How many riders recognise what the balance should be? How many have sufficient balance themselves? And finally, how many have the ability to change the balance appropriate to what is required of the horse?

ON THE AIDS

The next question is perhaps the most important of all. How many appreciate that the 'perfect balance' expected of a horse on the aids is actually something most refined? Not only does it take years to achieve but, even when attainable, everything is in a permanent state of flux, requiring minute adjustments at any given moment. Perfect balance is precarious. It is in the moment.

The longer I have taught riders on their own or my horses, the more I have realised that a supple, balanced horse depends upon a supple, balanced rider.

LEFT Prazer in his first year of training, aged six. This is the typical balance of the novice horse as he takes the bit forward within the framework of our aids which merely guide but never restrict.

BELOW Prazer at fourteen in levade. Only after years of bend and stretch exercises will the horse – like a ballet dancer – develop the strength and flexibility to sustain the balance of the higher airs.

The most highly trained horse in the world can be unbalanced by an imperfect rider – generally, more so. In other words, the marvellous potential of the horse to display beautiful, pure movement can be marred by something as simple as the rider's legs 'aiding' in the wrong place, a hand blocking or a seat bone incorrectly weighted.

FINDING THE CENTRE

Many books have been written with complex descriptions of the horse's centre of gravity and how it moves forward and back for different requirements. How do we recognise the difference? This will come with experience, but more important at the onset must be to try to merge our own balance with that of the horse in everything he does.

In the early days we follow the horse as best we can without letting him 'fall apart' or lean too much on the forehand. Once he is stronger, we take the lead by setting up the desired balance ourselves and then inviting the horse to balance around us. This is the idea behind the term 'to centre'. Done tactfully and gradually, it transforms the partnership.

Here, a discreet 'check' through my core, over the horse's centre of gravity, sets Q back on her hocks to lighten the forehand – prior to going forward again.

Dealing with the first stage on a young or uneducated horse, we should inter-fere as little as possible. We simply allow the horse to move 'through' us in a free, forward and relaxed way. Riders need constant reminding that the young horse relies on his head and neck for balance, with just enough elastic contact to discourage leaning. At this early stage of training, there will be considerably more weight over the forelegs – in other words, the horse is more balanced on his shoulders than on his quarters. This is natural, normal and to be expected.

Here, the rider actively encourages the young horse to stretch his neck forward correctly, without letting him 'fall apart'. Note the giving fingers and elbows as the leg encourages longer strides.

WEIGHT BACK

As the horse progresses in his training, the idea is to encourage the horse to move off his forehand and towards a horizontal balance. This is important if we want the horse to carry us easily and to move as Nature intended. The muscles and ligaments required to support the joints in this improved balance will take time to develop and there are no quick fixes. Instead a programme of strategic training – as in training a ballet dancer – must be adopted. The time put in will prolong the horse's life and fitness levels immeasurably.

The various dressage movements are designed to teach the horse to step more under himself: circles and turns to start, lateral work at a later stage.

The 90 degree turn is one of the first exercises to teach the horse to push from behind. Note the guidance of the rider's outside leg, while the outside rein allows forward for the neck to lengthen.

As the centre of gravity shifts sideways, it is the job of the inside hind to step underneath, bend and support it. By working quietly and progressively on both reins, the horse learns to engage each hind leg in turn, thus transferring weight to the rear.

Depending on temperament and ability, it may be two or three years before the horse is ready for an Elementary level dressage test. By this stage, the load on the horse's forelegs should have gradually shifted further back. The ideal (according to Seunig) is when 45 per cent of the combined horse/rider weight is eventually carried on the haunches and hind legs. More than that is inadvisable, although in certain High School movements, up to 100 per cent of the horse's weight is momentarily transferred to the hind end.

Once we have achieved lateral suppling, longitudinal suppling – over the back – will follow. It cannot be stressed too often how progressive work of this nature takes patience and, above all – time.

For this reason the young horse whose main job is simply to go forward must never be expected to come fully on the bit; until he has developed strength and engagement behind.

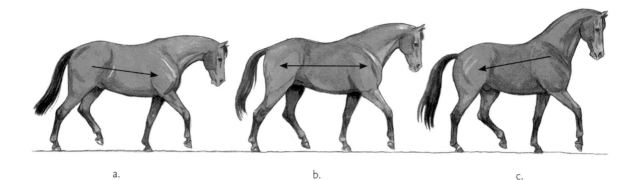

ABOVE In dressage, the different balances of the ridden horse
will be translated in terms such as these: (a) 'on the forehand'
(b) 'evenly balanced' (c) 'on the hocks'

UNEVENNESS

When we see a crooked horse, it is usually because one hind leg is less able to
bend and bear weight as efficiently as the other. If this state of affairs is not
helped in the early days, the horse will always favour one side more than the
other and later the riding of movements will become increasingly difficult on
the weaker rein. Generally, horses find it harder to bear weight on the right
hind, either for conformational reasons or because the majority of riders sit
heavier to this side and may block the engagement of the right hind.

In time and with patience – nothing must be forced – things should gradually even up, and horses can be easier to correct than most humans. However,
neither species is totally ambidextrous!

SUPPLING EXERCISES

As more and more exercises are introduced, the centre of gravity continues
to shift further to the rear as the horse grows in strength and flexibility. The
rider must be conscious of using each and every movement as a building block,
always returning to basics in between. Any natural inconsistency will tend to
disappear once these become part and parcel of the training programme.

With time, it is not only the hocks and fetlocks that bend to a greater
degree; the angles of the stifle and hip begin to close too. The deeper the
haunches, the more the forehand will rise, taking the head with it. Raising
the horse's head with the hand alone is a fruitless exercise, since until the
horse has deepened behind, he will continue on the forehand and be forced to

Suppling work on the circle encourages the inside hind to step under and take weight behind. Drop your inside leg by the girth so the horse wants to bend into and around it. Try this on loose reins too.

BELOW Pressure into the inside stirrup invites the horse to bend and move off the track while the hands appear to do nothing. Note the forward reach of the inside hind.

hollow under saddle. Only from sufficiently engaged hocks will the horse flex naturally through the atlas-occipital joint, generally referred to as the poll. Softening and yielding to the bit has a rebound effect throughout his body.

HAND RIDING

When riders rely on the reins for their own balance, they can impinge so much on the horse's natural carriage that crookedness may again ensue. Instead of smooth, flowing gaits, we see erratic movement and bridle lameness.

On the subject of contact – see Chapter 3 – it seems that many riding schools readily teach how to take, but there is less emphasis on how to give. Without the 'give' moment in every stride, too much tension in the rein may block the horse's shoulder as it moves forward. This will affect the length of stride in the affected foreleg.

Confusion reigns about what contact actually is, let alone how much or how little is required for a horse to function correctly. As for the different rein effects (to be discussed) they remain widely unknown – although good riders often use them quite naturally.

BELOW, LEFT To push the horse back out to the track, the inside leg will act against the horse's body. Note the engagement of the inside hind which renders the horse light in hand.

BELOW, RIGHT Be generous to reward every correct response so the horse can relax his jaw and stretch those hardworking muscles and joints. 'Open the hands, open the horse!'

What must always be made clear it that no horse can be expected to come to the bit – or remain on the bit – until he has learned to take his weight back.

ON THE BIT

There are two types of flexion, direct and indirect – see Chapters 3 and 4 – which lead to a feeling of lightness in the rider's hand. With less reliance on the reins for support, the horse is able to sustain a roughly horizontal balance for longer periods, but may still drop onto the forehand when he is tired. For this reason, we must work him gradually with frequent stretch periods, until the 'on the bit' position becomes natural and sustainable.

Whilst many riders believe they are riding on the bit when the horse is overbent, the FEI (Fédération Equestre Internationale) Dressage Rules are unequivocal. They stipulate that the horse's head should be just in front of the vertical, with the poll the highest point of the neck. This indicates an angle of roughly 90 degrees from poll to jaw, and – assuming that the horse remains in the horizontal – 90 degrees to the ground. This degree of flexion does not happen overnight. Again, it requires a progressive suppling of the entire body – particularly from behind the saddle.

Once the horse has learned to bend, yield or 'let go' from the poll, the relaxation of the jaw follows naturally. This is not so much an individual action of the lower jaw; rather that the horse simply accepts the bridle and does not resist it by trying to push in the opposite direction from the rider's hands. As with humans, clamped jaws induce tension elsewhere. Overly tight nosebands are highly counterproductive; not only do they cause pain and resistance, but they restrict the horse's breathing. The FEI prescribes a gentle 'champing' of the bit and it is most important that the horse can move his tongue and keep his mouth moist and compliant if he is to continue in this vein. This is very different from a mouth that 'yaws' open when pain is applied to the bars of the mouth or worse, the tongue.

IN FRONT OF THE VERTICAL

Clearly, the angle of the horse's head will appear to change once the horse is no longer horizontal to the ground. A very collected horse will be deeper behind, with a higher forehand, so even though the head is still in the accepted 'on the bit' position, it will be in front of the vertical. A typical example would be in the upward phase of canter, in the pirouette, or in a good piaffe. In such a case, the 90 degree angle from poll to jaw has not changed at all, but the body that carries it has. The deeper the haunches, the more the forehand will rise, taking the head with it. This is of course biomechanically correct and should *never* be condemned in a dressage test – judges beware!

(The above scenario should never be confused with a horse on the forehand, whose head is too high, or who is simply resisting the bridle by pushing up from the brachiocephalic muscle under his neck.)

In the upward phase of canter, the more engaged the horse, the more the horse's nose will appear in front of the vertical. This is biomechanically correct, commensurate with the degree of collection.

In the downward phase of canter, there may be a moment when the withers are lower than the quarters. In such an event, the horse's nose may appear behind the vertical without any change in the length of rein.

Stretching the horse on the longer rein is not the same as giving the reins completely as in 'free walk'. A happy forward thinking horse will continue to seek the contact of our hand by taking the head forward and down. Look for the wither connecting into the neck in one long, rounded arch. The lower the head the more it will appear BTV despite the angle being opened well beyond 90 degrees.

BEHIND THE VERTICAL (BTV)

In the downward phase of canter, we have the reverse situation. As the haunches lift and the shoulders come down, the horse may still flex correctly from the poll, but the head may momentarily appear behind the vertical – but this should not be viewed as a fault unless the rein contact has been shortened. The same can happen with a novice horse who is still a little on the forehand.

We have a similar situation when the horse is being worked forward and down into the long rein to encourage stretch. The lower the neck, the more the head will seem to 'move' behind the vertical so long as he seeks the contact of the rider's hand. Even when the angle from nose to poll is opened well beyond the 90 degree point the head will be BTV.

Bad BTV is when the head is pulled towards the horse's body because the neck has been shortened – a very different scenario.

When the poll has yielded as far as it can, the horse is then forced to 'break' between the second and third vertebrae. This form of 'rounding' stresses the ligaments around the wither, interrupts the play of the longdissimus back muscles with connectivity lost behind. Look out for a tell-tale hollow at the base of the neck.

ROUNDING

I believe a lot of the confusion in these matters comes from people's interpretation of roundness. Real roundness must come from behind – the result of:

- well-engaged hocks
- a supple croup
- a softly raised back
- lifting of the shoulders
- a raised, arched neck
- poll the highest point

BELOW Real roundness should be present over the entire silhouette – the result of good, even muscle tone and well engaged and flexible hindlimb joints.

All of these indicate the forward stretching of the horse into a naturally rounded shape. Instead, the opposite has become the fashion – a shrinking down or contraction of the horse's outline into an artificial shape.

Such is the current fashion for misconstrued 'roundness' or 'downhill' riding, that the desirable and natural lifting of the forehand seems misunderstood and is no longer favoured as in years gone by. This points to general ignorance all round about how horses move.

It is very sad for horses that many of today's riders are lured into thinking that a horse cannot be 'round' unless the head and neck are pulled in. This is BTV gone mad!

CORRECTIVE SCHOOLING

Working long and low can help build muscle on horses who are very hollow and resistant, but only if conducted on a light rein. This form of schooling is only 'corrective' *when the horse is able to lengthen his neck as he arches and stretches down and forward into hands that know how much to take and give.* This will naturally raise the back as the hind legs come further underneath to support him, not the bit! Exercising the horse in this way should only be done for a few minutes at a time, before returning to normal.

More common is the horse who is stiff and heavy on the forehand. In this case riding deep will only exacerbate the problem. Instead, teach the horse to go forward on a light rein. Allow him to be responsible for his own balance! After that, suppling exercises which teach the horse to engage and step under behind will have an immediate and beneficial effect.

FORCE

Too many riders expect the horse to bend through the poll before he is supple enough to do so. Forcing the head into the vertical with a gadget or taut reins will only shorten the neck and bend it halfway down the crest instead of flexing from the poll. This not only places the head behind the vertical but teaches the horse to be heavy in the hands.

Overbending in this way places enormous stress on the delicate neck ligaments. A common sign of forcing or pulling back with the rein is a telltale hollow in the trapezius area just in front of the withers. Although the horse's back may be raised, the correct interplay of the muscle fibres is blocked, which may lead to deterioration and spasm.

NOSE-POKING

A degree of nose-poking in the youngster is a natural process which should gradually disappear once the horse is more supple. Clearly, if the hind legs are not strong enough to support the back, there will be hollowing to start, including a concave neck. All this will improve as the horse learns to work from behind.

In the case of the mature horse persistently pushing his nose up to resist the rein, we should explore further. This may represent a *cri de coeur*. It suggests that something is hurting. Backs and teeth are the first things to be checked, but uneducated hands, the wrong bit or the rider sitting heavily over the sensitive loin area are frequent causes.

This horse is perfectly sound and strong, but he has never previously been asked to come onto the bit. He is therefore difficult to control in trot and canter. With his head in this angle, it is very easy to take off – which he regularly does! The rider sits nicely but is ineffectual.

In the case of the above photo there are no physical problems and the horse is simply used to this way of going like many horses. All the rider has to do to drop her horse's nose, is sit up taller, square her shoulders and close her legs at the girth. Immediately, the horse rewards her by flexing through the poll and bending around her leg as he moves off the track – see overleaf.

Such a simple manoeuvre with such a dramatic result can be the begining of a journey to self improvement and finding the right balance for you and the horse.

Once the horse has learned to soften through the poll and jaw, every joint in his body begins to yield. Start in walk and let the horse feel the difference and offer his back. Gradually he will learn to do this in all three gaits.

There is all the difference in the world between evasive nose-poking and the sight of a correctly flexed horse carrying his head in front of the vertical. At the risk of stating the obvious, the main purpose of every exercise, every dressage movement is the raising of the horse's forehand, the product of good engagement behind.

LIGHTNESS

For the High School horse engaged in display work this higher balance is very desirable. It allows the horse to balance more on the hocks, and to twist, turn and move sideways with the greatest of ease. The higher the forehand, the more pivotal the movement and it is from this balance that the whole idea of lightness emanates.

All this shows that the word 'balance' can mean different things to different people.

Generally however, it should be possible to school all horses to a degree of balance whereby the slightest aid is understood by the horse, and where the horse can react to that aid easily and comfortably.

I always remember the words of William Golding in one of his novels where he describes 'the fragility of beauty'. For me, that sums up riding! The horse's balance is a very fragile and beautiful thing. It cannot be fixed or constrained; it is arrived at in a moment of utter grace and poise – a special insight in a special moment.

It's a very special thing when the horse gives his balance to us. We have to earn it by riding quietly and correctly with aids that help, never detract from the beauty of each God-given natural movement.

CLASSICAL QUOTES

'The young horse should be allowed to carry its head and neck in a position that's as free as possible.'

— HEUSCHMANN, GERMAN SCHOOL

✦

'Good hands are essential to help the horse discover the strength to balance himself without outside support.'

— BURGER, GERMAN SCHOOL

✦

'Carriage or bearing will always vary, and must correspond to the degree of dressage [training] and to the character and conformation of the horse.'

— MÜSELER, GERMAN SCHOOL

✦

'The more the horse's hindquarters move underneath him, the further back the centre of gravity moves.'

— BLIGNAULT, SOUTH AFRICAN SCHOOL

✦

'A horse that is psychologically and bodily cramped will find it hard to flex and relax its muscles elastically and in a relaxed state.'

— SEUNIG, GERMAN SCHOOL

✦

'Not every horse can be given a head position bordering on the vertical. Certain ones can only be put in hand after great difficulty.'

— OLIVEIRA, PORTUGUESE SCHOOL

'The head alone being raised will not make a horse light.'

— PETERS, ENGLISH SCHOOL

✦

'Necks that are pulled in stop the muscles of the back developing and interfere with the natural paces.'

— KLIMKE, GERMAN SCHOOL

✦

'Isn't it quite apparent that horses that lean on the bit are almost always more or less on their shoulders, whereas horses that refuse to take "support" are more or less balanced on their haunches?'

— PAILLARD, SCHOOL OF SAUMUR

THE AIDS
FOR IMPULSION

Forward and Straight

Calm, active, forward and straight![1]

THIS HAS BEEN THE mantra at The Spanish Riding School of Vienna for many years.[1] It is the underlying principle for all forms of equitation. But how many people actually give the correct aids to motivate the horse to be full of impulsion yet straight and calm at all times?

Out hacking it is much easier to complement the horse for what we expect him to do. By adopting the forward seat, we take pressure off the back, the loins are released and the hindquarters can develop greater forward-driving power. At speed, or cross-country, crouching over the withers allows the horse to stretch his frame and unite his balance with ours. The horse will generally want to follow our weight whatever he is doing.

NON-INVASIVE RIDING

Things become more complex when we want to do dressage. In his first year, the young dressage horse will naturally be on the forehand so again, a light, forward seat will complement the balance. There must be no attempt to fix the head position, just maintain a feel. It is much easier to weight the stirrups

---

1 The maxim is based upon the original phrase of the French Master, L'Hotte: 'Calm, forward and straight'.

In the early days we want the young horse to stretch forward into the contact. To keep him in balance, think more 'up' and vertical in your rising. This helps you to use your core to influence the gait rather than resist through the hands.

correctly when we are off the horse's back. In this way, we encourage the horse to reach forward into an allowing elastic contact as described in the previous chapter.

RISING TROT

'Posting' to the trot has several advantages. First, it relieves the horse's back of unwanted pressure and takes our own energy forward. Once the horse has learned to maintain a good steady rhythm, he will want to marry up with us. We may then use the rising trot either to allow a little more or, indeed, to block any tendency to rush.

Second, rising trot allows the equine dorsal muscles to contract and stretch without impediment. This allows the horse full use of the hind leg extensor muscles so vital for covering the ground and the potential of the gait. Thus the dynamic balance of horse and rider together is much improved.

Third and equally important, rising allows the rider to remain stable or 'grounded' with their weight carried over the strongest part of the horse's back from whence the stirrups are slung. It is easy then to weight them equally for

In the sitting trot, keep the waist forward and the shoulders back for extra core support. Let the legs drop so the horse can move through the channel of your aids.

riding forward in straight lines. Happily too, the rider's legs should naturally be positioned closer to the girth to assist the horse in his forward progression. (It is almost impossible to rise in balance with the legs too far back.)

SITTING TROT

Gradually, as the horse learns to carry more weight behind, we can start to adopt a more upright central position. The classical seat, with vertical pelvis and seat bones in the middle of the saddle, allows us to control our own weight and that of the horse at will – but how many people do this effectively? At the same time, how may we ensure that the horse remains forward-thinking in all that we do?

READY TO GO

Take the stationary horse. You have just mounted and he stands, roughly square, awaiting your first command. Most of us just think 'forward' and a forward-going horse will comply. Others need a little more persuasion. Is this their fault, or could it be ours? Are we asking correctly, so the horse moves forward and straight with energy – for example, from halt to trot in a dressage test?

Before we even think about using our legs, we should sit up. This immediately frees the horse from unwanted pressure and allows the legs to act without restriction. For an immediate response, apply both legs together, lightly and swiftly. For medium or extended walk, the legs should act alternately, swinging in time with the rhythm. Apart from canter, the legs are at their most

Always sit up and drop the legs once halt is achieved. This will make it easier to remain immobile and for your horse to move forward with his back up the moment you ask with both legs at the girth.

Progressing to medium trot, I always think 'shoulders back' to project my energy up and forward. A swift 'asking' close of both legs at the girth helps lift the withers, but don't sit heavy!

effective when both are applied *at the girth*.[2] A couple of gentle taps, or a quick nip followed by an immediate release, generally stimulates the horse's interest. Always wait for a response, before asking again. There is no place in the school for kicking.

With the ticklish, anxious or sensitive horse, the forward aid may need to be dampened down. Think of closing the leg at the girth very softly. With tact and progressive reinforcement, even the most excitable horse can be trained to accept the leg.

MULTI-TASKING

Never forget that the legs have many roles and that saying 'forward' is only one of them.

What riders must learn to do is distinguish between the leg aids. You cannot expect your horse to react correctly to any aid until you know:

- how to use them

- where to use them

- when to use them and – most important –

- when not to use them.

---

2 Please note for future reference, the expression 'leg at the girth' generally suggests that the rider's toe is aligned with the girth, not the heel – except perhaps in lengthening.

Most riders think they should be applied in every stride. This is most definitely not the case. Instead they must ask – *then cease their action to allow* – before acting again. In this way, we gradually reinforce the message that the horse did the right thing.

But is that enough? If the rider does not also 'release' or 'allow' through the hands, seat and upper body, the legs may work all they like – but to little effect. No horse will want to go forward if we sit like a sack of potatoes and particularly if the legs act in the wrong place.

HEAD-HIP-HEEL ALIGNMENT (HHHA)

Once in motion, matching up bits of the body is a favourite preoccupation of certain instructors. This is not always as helpful as most people think. While the principle is excellent for being lunged – i.e. to open the joints – for collection or for halt – most exercises demand that our legs vary their position. These changes, however small, alter the effect of our weight on the horse's back.

Few appear to appreciate that the HHH line can only be valid if the seat remains in the correct position – i.e. in the middle of the saddle. When the rider drifts towards the cantle – as is too often seen – things go badly wrong.

BELOW, LEFT Inviting the horse to extend the walk, I give alternate leg aids to amplify the gait. Note – the position of my right leg is too far back for normal work.

BELOW, RIGHT To pick up the forehand for a more 'uphill' collected walk, a quick press on the 'accelerator' close to the girth, does wonders.

Not only does the horse struggle, the rider may struggle to keep their balance. Clichés should be treated with caution!

OPPOSITE FEEL

To make us more precise, remember that the legs (as well as the seat and upper body) have a controlling effect on the horse's energy. In addition to saying 'forward', they can also slow, halt, collect or invite the horse into rein-back.

If the leg at the girth is key to forward impulsion, taking both legs behind the girth will radically change the *feel*. Horses are much more sensitive to these adjustments than people realise and again some knowledge of biomechanics is helpful. Basically, legs applied well behind the girth pull the front of the rider's pelvis forward and down. In other words, this posture tips the balance. This may have a positive or negative effect. An educated horse may adapt accordingly.[3] A lazy horse will generally get slower, and a sensitive horse will probably stop! This is hardly surprising, when we have effectively 'closed the door'.

---

3 At advanced levels, taking the legs back is also used in the more collected movements such as piaffe and passage – where forward impulsion is diverted upward – see Chapter 11.

'Closing the door' in front, opens it behind for the horse to step back easily. Keep the horse's neck arching forward with just a light feel on the rein to invite the weight and energy back.

ON-OFF!

Clearly, without energy we can do nothing with our horses. Visualisation is a great tool, so think of impulsion like electricity. It's quick – it's instant. Think of switching on a light bulb. Sit up and energise yourself! Open hips allow your weight to fall away from you, flow down over the front of the thigh, keeping you deep and centred in the saddle without constriction.

Think 'up and forward 'before you apply a quick, effective 'ask'. If your horse is very sensitive, this may be no more than a 'breath' from the lower leg. What's important here is that a tap or pinch – firm or gentle – requires you to open the joints. It's a very different feeling from a prolonged squeeze, or worse a kick. *One stimulates, the other inhibits.*

If the horse is reluctant and you have given him the chance to react, simply ask again. Initially, a quick touch of the stick – behind the boot – to simulate the leg aid is better by far than stronger aids. Always be quick to drop your legs the second the horse responds – even if this sequence has to be repeated again and again. Each time he moves forward, *take the pressure off.* Believe he will go forward. *Let* him go forward!

A quick close or 'ask' for forwardness may be done via the top of the boot on a sensitive horse or further down the shin. Unless the knee is deep and the thigh turned in, the forward aid will be ineffectual.

SWITCHED OFF

It is tragic to hear of horses 'dead to the leg'. This can be caused by an unbalanced body, unyielding hands or unyielding legs. Baucher, the great nineteenth-century French Master, wrote of 'hand without legs – legs without hand' which has helped countless learner riders to think before they act. Clearly anyone who drives their horses into an unremitting contact will gradually destroy the will of the horse to go forward.

Nevertheless, this saying should not be taken to an extreme[4] since the hands must always receive the forward impulse, but the idea of a nano-second between the 'ask' and receive, or the 'ask' and give is a positive one.

SADDLES

The conscientious rider must beware of saddles that fix the seat and legs into a certain position and may in fact 'close the door'. This can happen with very overstuffed saddles or those where the stirrup bars are set too far back. Always choose a saddle which allows you total freedom through the hip joint to move your (whole) leg forward and back as appropriate – and that includes the thigh. Only with open hips can you release the horse from unwanted pressure – all of which inhibits impulsion.

LET GRAVITY WORK FOR YOU

Remember the horse is ruled by the same rules of gravity as we are, so with the legs in a neutral, hanging but toned position – roughly at the girth – it is comparatively easy for the rider to stay in balance. For riding straight lines, the weight in each seat bone, each stirrup will be roughly 50:50, but we should naturally deepen the weight into the inside stirrup for a corner, bend or turn as discussed in more detail later.

---

4 This quotation is often taken too literally. Baucher used it to explain that the hands must not contradict the forward aid of the legs and that is the spirit in which it should be interpreted. There have been hundreds of discussions and arguments both amongst his pupils and latter-day experts as to the nuances of training, both in Baucher's first manner and his second manner. Most generally agree, that the use of hand and legs must co-operate with each other and, as the horse progresses to a higher stage, it is almost impossible to separate the aids since all will be operating in delightful concert with each other. For further reading on the subject see *Racinet Explains Baucher*, Xenophon Press.

Sitting tall and well up to the pommel allows my hips to open naturally, so the legs fall into place. Tone not tension is the name of the game.

Without core support, it can be hard to remain vertical in movement. A sloppy upper body position weakens the stabilising effect of gravity. An upright posture allows the legs to *hang* at the girth, not by force but by gravity alone. In this position, the legs provide clear guidelines to keep the horse travelling forward and in the required direction. Equally importantly, we have 'opened the door' to the horse's energy. We sit up, square the shoulders, the legs 'ask' at the girth and the horse respond as they drop. Quick march!

LINE UP!

Basically, the forward aids should now comprise a channel made up of both reins and both legs to send the horse forward and *through*. Our hips and shoulders must be level and aligned to his. It takes concentration to keep everything

Like the centaur, Q and I remain 'lined up' in the same direction, same angle, same attitude one to another, drawing support and energy one from the other.

even, flowing and harmonious. Most of us are naturally one-sided so we have to be especially vigilant on our less favoured rein.

Something as simple as a turned-out knee or 'leaving a shoulder behind' may provide an escape route for the horse's energy, yet this is easily corrected by looking between the horse's ears. Visual help is our most natural aid; yet in riding it is often overlooked. Looking ahead sends a message to the brain so that, without over-aiding, you and the horse can move 'as one piece'. Correct any 'slippage' by keeping the buttons of your jacket lined up with the horse's mane at all times.

MAINTAINING IMPULSION

Horses move in spite of us, not because of us. The more we interfere, the less they go forward. Don't nag! The best work is when the rider sits tall and appears to do nothing – but mentally, of course, that is never the case.

THE AIDS FOR IMPULSION

Motivate your horse by varying the work. Never neglect the walk, it helps to calm and balance the hot horse; combined with transitions, it will energise the phlegmatic. Whether you turn, circle, go sideways, change the rein, modify the gait, stop, start or move backwards – make everything you do a conscious decision. There is nothing more boring for horse and rider than going round and round the school or round and round the same old circle in the same gait.

Decide what you wish to do, look through the ears at all times, imagine an arc of energy moving over the horse's back, neck and into your hands and enjoy it! Once *you* lighten up, so will your horse.

THINGS TO GUARD AGAINST

There is a big difference between tension and tone. Any form of squeezing with the leg narrows 'the gap', so there is less motivation for the horse to move forward and *through*.

Never over-correct. Constant repetition does not make perfect. Go and do something else and surprise yourself!

THINK POSITIVE

If you become discerning with your legs, the time will come when you scarcely have to repeat that first forward request in a particular session. It's a great moment when, having been asked for trot, the horse stays trotting with the same frame, the same energy and your legs just hang – breathing with the horse in every stride. You are on your way!

CLASSICAL QUOTES

'Since any healthy horse is capable of impulsion, and good impulsion, it is up to you to convince him that your demands are reasonable.... Leg action must be clear-cut, its vigour adapted to the horse's sensitivity, insist on his advancing freely at the very first touch.'

— FROISSARD, FRENCH SCHOOL

✦

'If a judge notices that a horse is not perfectly straight but it goes with impulsion, stretches the reins lightly but positively and obeys his rider's indications promptly and calmly, he should not attach too much importance to a slight degree of crookedness.'

— ALBRECHT, SCHOOL OF VIENNA

✦

'The greatest difficulty arises with horses who run away because they cannot bear the leg.'

— MÜSELER, GERMAN SCHOOL

✦

'The effect of using both legs by the girth is to encourage the horse to move forward. This is the basis of all training and is developed and refined by constant repetition, until the slightest pressure with the inside of the rider's legs will result in the horse moving forward.'

— PRINT, ENGLISH SCHOOL

✦

'Impulsion is the condition whereby a horse's propelling forces are constantly at the disposal of its rider for the immediate and generous execution of any requested movement.'

— PAILLARD, SCHOOL OF SAUMUR

'The moment the horse obeys, the legs remove their pressure and the fingers also ease their pressure on the reins; the legs and the hands do not renew their action unless the head retakes of itself a defective position.'

— BLACQUE BELLAIR, FRENCH SCHOOL

✦

'Practise, as often as possible, reducing or ceasing the forward aid completely with your legs.'

— KOTTAS, SCHOOL OF VIENNA

✦

'We should arrive at a point where the rider's legs serve only to give the necessary impulsion to the exercise in progress, and intervene solely again when the rider wishes to go on to a new exercise.'

— OLIVEIRA, PORTUGUESE SCHOOL

REIN AIDS

Ask and Give; Direct Flexion and Stretch

Subtlety with the rider's hand is something that is often neglected even in higher-level dressage today. For some the only way to ride a horse is to steer from the front end, rather like riding a bicycle. As for the different rein effects discussed here and thereafter, they seem rarely mentioned, although good riders will use them quite unconsciously.

At this stage, we are only concerned with the first rein effect – that of the direct or opening rein, which indicates to the horse to turn into it. This may be done by a mere feel of the fingers, either by rotating the wrist so the fingernails show uppermost or, in the case of the younger horse, moving the hand slightly outward – away from the horse's neck. *The opening hand should never ever pull back.*

CONTACT

There is also confusion about the word 'contact'. I am often asked by my students what contact actually is – which I find worrying. As I wrote in my first book on dressage, *The Classical Seat*, 'Contact is quite simply

Whether going straight or asking for bend, the hands should remain opposite each other, with just a soft feel through the fingers.

Good contact depends upon a quiet and stable seat. There must be an unbroken, harmonious line from the horse's mouth via the rider's hands through the wrists to the elbow. The easing of the rider's joints including those of the back, shoulders and hips allow us to retain this connection without appearing to do anything.

the link between the rider's hands and the horse's mouth.' Good contact has nothing to do with pulling or how many pounds of weight you carry in your hand.

The main role of the hands is to act as a receiver or regulator for the horse's energy that the seat and legs have encouraged or produced, and to allow it through in its forward progression. Their other role is of course to re-channel or redirect. At all times they should reconfirm the aids of the rider's body.

The amount of contact will vary considerably from horse to horse. It should be constant but allowing with the newly backed horse; firmer with the novice horse – whose balance may be faulty and who will need more support – and grow lighter by stages with the advanced horse. And herein lies the great myth about contact. For dressage, we should *not* be riding around with washing-line reins except in the stretch or, for a few moments, in a *descente de main* (see Chapter 12). *Instead, it should be the horse who begins to lighten on the rein, not the rider who abandons the contact.* A well-schooled, connected horse should make his own lightness as a result of superior engagement.

Drop the hand to encourage the free walk where the horse can stretch his head and neck as much as he desires. Keep the back supported as much as possible with the leg at the girth.

RESPECT FOR THE MOUTH

Contact can only be maintained comfortably if the rider has as an acute aware-ness of how the horse is reacting to the bit (or bits) in his mouth. The type of bit used may need to be changed as the horse progresses in his education.

I always ask my students to visualise the inside of the horse's mouth. People need to become more aware of the soft, fleshy tongue, the tender skin around the bars of the mouth, and the sensitive palate where a nutcracker snaffle or a high port can cause real pain. Where a mouth is particularly narrow or the palate low, never hesitate to take professional advice.

Generally, the reins should be held no further apart than the width of the bit. However, to encourage a young horse to lengthen his neck, we may open them more, which reduces the pressure on the bars of the mouth.

Riders need to have good balance and a well-confirmed seat in order to carry the hands quietly as a pair. The hands must never move back, either separately or together. To check or steady a rushing horse from the hands alone is frankly futile. Energy needs to be re-channelled from the centre – long before it reaches the forehand. We do this through the aids of our seat, legs and upper body. Quietly fixing the shoulders and elbows and pushing the core muscles forward towards a fixed hand helps resist a pulling horse.

LEFT Opening both hands on the young horse to encourage the stretch allows him to lower his neck whilst still retaining sufficient contact to keep his back up and his neck arching.

ABOVE The old maxim 'hands together, horse together' is oh, so true.

QUIET HANDS

Bridging the rein is a useful way to establish a quiet hand for both the novice rider and the advanced. For a particularly difficult movement, it helps stabilise the hands and allows both reins to lightly touch and frame the neck – an important aid in itself. It is also useful with a pulling horse, since he will find he is only pulling against himself.

If the rider's back is not erect and supple, the shoulders slump, the chest is restricted and the hands may block. There will be no 'allowing' feeling travelling down the rein to the horse's mouth. Tight hands lead to tightness elsewhere. The thumb secures the rein, but unless the horse is actively pulling, the fingers should be loosely bent around it. This is the only way to gently 'feel' the mouth in the time-honoured manner or indeed to regulate how much or how little energy we allow through, which will ultimately determine balance and outline.

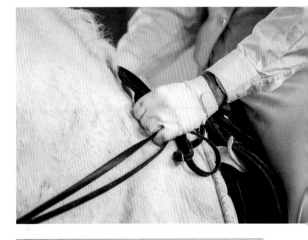

For a tricky movement, a hard or over-sensitive mouth, there is nothing wrong with bridging the reins which will spare the horse discomfort, should problems arise.

GIVE AND TAKE

There must obviously be an element of fixity about the wrists for the fingers to give and take on the rein if we are to communicate our wishes clearly to the horse. To describe those feelings that convey 'Yes, you may go!' or 'Please slow or collect!' is very personal. For me, the 'ask' is similar to squeezing or crumbling pastry, but in the next nano-second I am releasing the crumbs back onto the pastry board! It's as fine a feeling as that.

In both cases, as in any delicate work with the hands, the arms must be bent and the upper body and shoulders firm. It should go without saying that these actions of the fingers should be totally invisible to any onlooker.

WAIST TO HANDS

A good rider will never set up an independent movement of the hands alone except perhaps on the long rein. Instead the rider allows the hands to be carried forward with the rest of the body. By projecting the core – 'waist to hands' – the hands are supported. There is nothing wrong with hands that lightly touch the horse's neck from time to time for extra finesse.

NOSEBANDS

It should be pointed out that, where possible, most horses work better in a simple cavesson noseband. Flash nosebands do indeed have a remedial purpose but tightening these beyond the usual guide of 'two fingers comfortably underneath' can set up real trouble for the future. The more pressure we apply, the less likely we are to develop a relaxed, happy mouth – and breathing problems are common. Instead of the impulsion travelling forward to be accepted with compliance, there may be a blockage. This can lead to choppy gaits, resistance and even bridle lameness.

FLEXIONS

The horse can never submit fully to the rider's hand until we have persuaded him that it is more comfortable to yield to the bit. Once the horse has progressed past the early stages, we may progress from the steady, forward-thinking hand to a more feeling, asking hand.

Flexion simply means to bend, so we are looking for the horse to bend from the poll. There are two types of flexion, which may be offered singly or together:

In the double bridle, it is generally the little finger on the snaffle that asks for lateral flexion. Direct flexion is prompted via the curb but often the weight of the reins alone is sufficient.

- Direct flexion, where the horse drops his chin to 'nod' down in response to the action on the bit of both reins,

- Indirect or lateral flexion, where the horse can turn his head sideways in response to a single rein action to right or left.

To accompany the above, the horse should automatically flex or yield through his lower jaw. Known as 'bridling' in former times, this natural submission will only happen when the horse is relaxed in both mind and body.

The 'ask' for flexion consists of little more than finger pressure. With a light play on the rein, both forms of flexion are requested in stages. We must never forget that the natural position of a horse's head in freedom is reasonably high and well in front of the vertical, so it will take time and patience to persuade him to come fully onto the bit as described in Chapter 1. Some people prefer to teach flexions on the ground first, but the main thing is to do it very quietly and only ask for a little at a time.

Nuno Oliveira warns against raising the horse's head when dismounted except very slowly and progressively.[1] He quotes Steinbrecht's point that it is impulsion which gives the head and neck its correct position. This, of course, can only happen in movement. As André Jousseaume points out in *Progressive Equitation,* one must always take account of the horse's conformation.

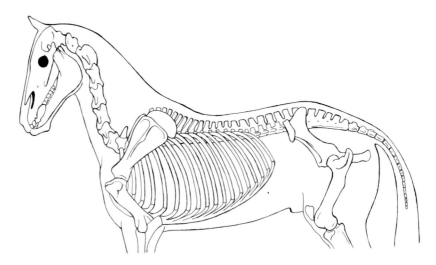

There is a limit to how much the horse can bend from the poll whether sideways or downward. As in the human, the skeletal processes only allow so much. Asking for more can severely impair the natural interplay of muscles and ligaments in the neck and back.

FORCE OR FEEL?

When gadgets are used to force the horse onto the bit, it is rare to see relaxation and flexion through the poll itself. As Karin Blignault points out in *Equine Biomechanics for Riders,* 'There is a restriction to the nodding and this is the limit of the "on the bit" [90 degree] position.' In other words, the poll can only bend so far.

When riders try to force the horse's head beyond that point, the horse has no alternative but to shorten and round the neck in order to flex behind the third and fourth vertebrae. Not only is the horse denied his vision but this unnatural posture leads to over-stretched ligaments, a compromised balance and general stresses and strain on the interverterbral joints and discs.

Instead, a good rider relies on the trust and responsiveness of the horse to an invitation. Opening and closing the fingers with a soft, gentle feel is similar to a delicate vibrato on the violin. Subtly done, from a steady wrist, it encourages the horse to yield when the poll is roughly the highest point of the neck and to relax the jaw, mouth the bit and salivate. Only then can beautiful music be made!

---

1 Decarpentry also made a cogent argument against attempting to do so mounted.

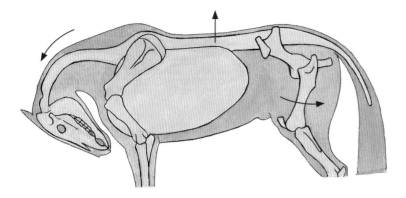

The practice of *rollkur* so prevalent in some riding schools and competition arenas is now thankfully being condemned by many vets, trainers and judges. Placing enormous pressures and strain on the entire locomotive system, 'hyperflexion', raises the back in the wrong areas and denies the horse of the ability to bend and mobilise his loins, haunches and hocks.

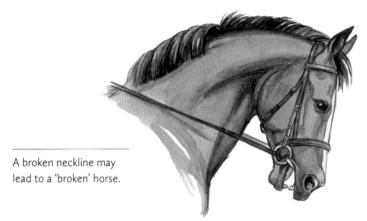

A broken neckline may lead to a 'broken' horse.

As the horse becomes stronger behind, it is much easier for him to maintain a naturally rounded frame. Horses learn to remain on the bit through a kind hand that knows when to give and when to take and through general conditioning. Positive reinforcement is everything. Resistances only occur when the rider has abused that trust, or demanded too much too soon.

It is important that the hand, wrist, forearm and elbow generally form one continuous line. The elbows must be bent for the joints to absorb movement and there must be no clamping of the upper arm against the rider's side. When we turn or rotate the hand for a particular request, the forearm must do the same. Any break in this line will result in a disruptive feeling in the horse's mouth.

LENGTHENING

When we wish the horse to lengthen his frame, we must be ready to ease the contact with the fingers the moment the horse responds to the forward drive of the legs. Then, depending on how much energy we wish to allow through,

Here Q's neck is arching nicely forward but for me the picture would be further improved with a fraction more give through my fingers. The extension of the forelegs is good and would please most dressage judges, but a little less extravagance in front and more from behind would be more technically correct.

we will continue to ease forward through the joints of the elbow, shoulder and lower back as we ask for bigger strides from behind. In this way the hand has the feeling of pushing the horse's energy back to him through the rein. Again, visualise the lengthening and project your own energy!

STRETCH

The stretch on the long rein must be introduced at regular intervals. During forty-five minutes of schooling, I would expect to give the younger horse a stretch every five or six minutes. With the mature horse, after about every eight to ten minutes of more collected, concentrated work.

Always keep the horse active from behind to support the back. Alternate leg aids that swing in the rhythm of the walk really help: leg on as the belly swings away, leg off as it moves into the leg. Do not push, but keep your back supple and think of a sideways feel through the hips as each seat bone is carried forward alternately.

Close and stretch exercises build up the strength of the horse until such time as he can remain on the bit in collection, or extend his body with ease and fluidity throughout.

THINGS TO GUARD AGAINST

Pulling back with the rein to one side or the other causes the rider to twist. Pulling back on both reins tightens the horse's neck, blocks the energy and places the horse on the forehand. If the horse 'falls' in or out on one shoulder, take the appropriate rein forward so he has nothing to lean on. This effectively encourages more engagement behind and corrects the balance.

THINK POSITIVE

In the classical French School, the *descente de main* (see Chapter 12) may either mean the complete surrender of the hand, or a momentary 'give' in the middle of a movement as a reward to a perfectly balanced horse. A well-schooled horse can often continue in this mode for several strides without any obvious loss of balance. With a novice horse, it is probably better initially to reward fully by returning to walk and allowing him to stretch. Whatever his level, get your horse used to being able to stand quietly on relaxed reins anywhere you choose in the school. This is a great way to instil confidence and also very practical for whatever you are doing!

CLASSICAL QUOTES

'The matter of contact greatly affects not only the mouth, the neck and the back, but the functioning of the hindlegs.'

— FROISSARD, FRENCH SCHOOL

✦

'With a new bit, let it be put in his mouth three or four mornings previous to your mounting him.'

— ASTLEY, ENGLISH SCHOOL

✦

'The correct contact with the bit may best be perceived when the rider rides on a loose rein at the walk or trot and takes up the reins again. There should not be any change in the rhythm or tempo of movement.'

— PODHAJSKY, SCHOOL OF VIENNA

✦

'Use the hands as little as possible if you want the horse to be as agreeable as possible.'

— LIÇART, SCHOOL OF SAUMUR

✦

'The hands remain quiet and passive whilst the horse maintains his attitude, forward thrust, his gait and the exercise. The hands will ask again only if there is a risk of change in the horse or if the rider wants to modify the exercise.'

— KOTTAS, SCHOOL OF VIENNA

✦

'Hands transmit messages from the rider's to the horse's brain via the animal's mouth and, unless the rider has a sympathetic understanding of the sensitivity of that mouth, he will hurt it.'

— WYNMALEN, DUTCH SCHOOL

✦

'In the first lesson of the action of the legs, the hand ought not to oppose the extension of the neck; on the contrary, the fingers should be half-open.'

— BLACQUE BELLAIR, FRENCH SCHOOL

✦

'When I say that flexions must be the trainer's first care, I really mean that they must be his first objective ... but there is not the slightest need to hurry flexions and harmonious ones at that, will appear all by themselves.'

— WYNMALEN, DUTCH SCHOOL

✦

'Remember that flexions in general, and particularly this one [direct flexion], are the result of relaxation, never forceful action .'

— FROISSARD, FRENCH SCHOOL

✦

'The fingering of the reins should regulate with absolute precision the distribution of the propulsion.'

— FILLIS, ENGLISH SCHOOL

THE ROLE OF THE INSIDE REIN AND INSIDE LEG

Lateral Flexion and Bend

THE SCALES OF TRAINING place straightness on the wish-list from the outset. Although fundamental to all training, this important objective is often taken out of context.

An idealistic view of straightness may place an expectancy on the part of riders and trainers alike to achieve the impossible without ever understanding the means to produce improvement. This is particularly true in the case of the novice horse. How many lessons do you see where horse and rider are drilled in so-called straight lines simply by going up and down the school time and again in walk, trot and canter? Often horse and rider end up tired, dispirited and stiff – which does nothing for forwardness and certainly not for straightness.

To me, this form of 'schooling' is madness. It depends on luck rather than common sense. How can the horse be straight until he has learned to soften and bend equally on both reins? Straightness requires real suppleness, a desire to move into the correct rein and a high degree of all round looseness and ambidexterity. Few horses will appear straight (particularly from behind) from the outset and for me, hacking is more beneficial than school drilling whenever possible for the young or novice horse.

LATERAL FLEXION

Once back in the school, it is generally accepted by Vienna and the French Classical School that, if the horse is to appear straight on the track or attempt any form of figure work, it is essential to ask for a degree of inside bend.

One of the hardest things for riders is to proceed straight down the centre-line in a dressage test. Eyes front and good posture is everything and generally the less we try to 'correct', the better.

This is because the quarters are wider than the shoulders and we need to place the forehand in line with the quarters. To do so means flexing the horse very gently in the direction of travel, even introducing a very slight feeling of shoulder-fore. Yielding to the inside and gently 'bending' in this way allows the horse to negotiate the school correctly, stepping deeper into the corners so he can remain 'out' to the track on straight lines. It also prevents any sense of falling in on circles and turns.

Once on the track, the horse will never appear straight without a degree of inside flexion. Even with the young horse, I must vibrate the inside rein just enough to see the glimmer of his eye. Gradually, I can then align the inside fore with the inside hind.

Inside flexion has to start with the poll if the horse is not to resist the requests of the inside leg. This requires no more than a gentle vibration on the inside rein (alone) so that the horse yields through the joint between the head and the first vertebra, the atlas.

As with direct flexion,[1] the action of the fingers must be subtle and the hands must still remain as a pair. At the same time, the rider's inside leg must similarly ask for bend with soft, light taps at the girth. Once bend is offered, try to drop the leg so it becomes a pillar of support.

---

1 Lateral flexion is sometimes referred to as 'indirect flexion' – as opposed to 'direct flexion'. This term should not be confused with the concept of the direct or indirect rein.

Always ride well *out* to the edge of the school. Remember your inside leg is a pillar! Watch for the shine of your horse's inside eye... and no more. Too much bend is as bad as too little.

If the inside leg is too strong, the horse may push against it rather than yielding into it. If it moves too much behind the girth, the forehand no longer feels supported and the horse may drop onto the forehand. Alternatively, he may move sideways (see Chapter 6).

For now, however, we are concerned with the horse travelling forwards so that the hind feet step into the prints of the forefeet. The impression of bend on turns and circles is produced by the horse lifting and tilting the ribcage away from gently applied pressure. Automatically, the centre of gravity moves outwards. The more schooled the horse, the more the inside fore and hind legs abduct and the more comfortable the ride.

It helps to think of each corner of the school as part of a circle – but the rider must guard against bending the horse's neck any more than the rest of his body. The concept of riding 'inside leg to outside rein' will be discussed in detail in the next chapter, but too much bend is as destructive to the general balance of the horse as too little.

With a very young horse, it may be helpful to open the inside hand when we wish to bend or turn, but overdone this can overload the inside

With the older horse, ride deep into your corners which will promote flexibility and straightness. At this point, your 'pillar' may have to issue a quick reminder at the girth. Guard against allowing it to stray back or the horse will lean into you.

shoulder. Within a few weeks however, a soft squeeze of the fingers alone should be recognised, so that both hands may remain quietly in place at the base of the neck.

HOW MUCH?

It is easy to test that you have the correct degree of bend. We should see no more than the glimmer of the horse's (inside) eye and the flare of his nostril. Any more is too much. Always watch your horse, as only in this way can you make checks or corrections to your own body.

There is no need to compromise your posture when you do this. Riders, like the horse, should deport themselves with poise and elegance. One of the worst habits of riders is to poke their head forward, resulting in a tight jaw and locked neck, which will be mimicked by the horse. Keep the back of your neck in contact with your collar when you ride, stretch tall through the crown and keep your chin relaxed and down. In the turn, continue to look through the horse's ears, and the time will come when he will bend or turn or even change legs from your eyes alone!

HIPS TO HORSE'S HIPS

The leg aids for bend are equally important. To enable the inside leg to 'hang' in the correct place – ready to ask or support – we must ensure that the inside hip remains slightly in advance of its opposite number on a bend or turn. The tighter the manoeuvre, the more we will become aware of this.

Advancing the inside hip and maintaining the leg on the girth for each exercise allows us to drop pressure into the inside stirrup without compromising upper body position. There must be no inclination to collapse the waist or lean. 'Lengthening' the inside leg, and stretching tall through the waist on the same side, makes it easier to weight the inside seat bone correctly. This will invite the horse to step under us more.

PILLAR OF SUPPORT

As well as supporting, the inside leg can also be a barrier – which says 'far enough!' In this way we keep the status quo – e.g. staying out to the track – staying out to the circle, (see section on Inside Leg to Outside Hand in

As we start a small circle my most important aid is inside hip forward, weight into inside seatbone (stirrup). There must be no pulling back with the inside rein which would badly compromise the horse's balance.

75

Chapter 5), etc. Once the horse becomes more attuned and develops greater suppleness, the inside leg can take on a more passive role. Nevertheless, it must be there. I always say to my students, 'Pillars don't move!'

As we prepare for tighter circles, turns and lateral work, the influence of the inside leg may be used to draw the horse in. This again requires the use of weight aids, to load the inside stirrup and seat bone to invite the horse deeper into the bend. Horses will always want to follow our weight.

A CLEAR INVITATION

Moving off the track the inside leg is now a magnet, drawing the horse towards the centre-line. As we start the canter half-pass, the inside hip must advance, leading horse and rider forward and sideways.

Gently weighting the inside stirrup in this way is particularly helpful in the canter depart. This gait will be described in more detail in Chapter 5, but suffice to say that applying a little more pressure into the ball of the right foot will help the horse to jump into the right lead. Since this action takes pressure off the rider's left seat bone, the outside hind is given greater freedom for the push-off.

For turning down the centre or quarter line, a similar aid is utilised. We simply sit up, deepen the knee and weight the inside stirrup through the ball of the foot. Provided the leg is not clamped against the horse's side, but hangs deep and quiet, the horse will want to move that way. This is another case of moving into pressure as the horse steps forward to find our inside leg. (It is the *opposite* feel of turn on the forehand where we push *against* the horse with the inside leg to move him in the opposite direction.)

To move the horse back out again we simply bring light pressure to bear against the horse's ribcage instead of dropping it down. None of this should change the position of the inside leg, which continues to remain at or just behind the girth.

The inside leg is a great straightening aid both in coming out of the turn or simply following a line. Again we see the importance of dropping weight into the stirrup with both knee and thigh snug to the saddle without gripping.

DUAL BENEFITS

Be aware therefore that the inside leg has a triple role. It may either:

- lead the horse inward, or

- nudge the horse outward

- keep the horse straight.

During both actions of the inside leg, the horse remains bent around it.

VARYING

With this idea in mind, we can vary the shape and size of our loops and circles or move the horse on or off the track at a moment's notice. The horse is very quick to pick up on these feelings as he is simply following our weight and yet it would be hard for anyone watching to spot the difference.

Even on slack reins, Prazer clearly wants to follow the weight aid of my inside leg. Remember this is pure physics; by tuning into gravity ourselves, we make everything so much easier for our horse.

Whilst the position of the inside leg remains roughly the same, the way in which we use pressure may vary as follows:

- To move straight ahead – keep both legs hanging roughly opposite the girth – equal pressure in each stirrup.

- To move in, we drop a little more pressure into the inside stirrup.

- To move out, we place a little more pressure against the horse's side and/ or transfer weight to the outside stirrup.

SHOULDER-FORE

Only when the horse is very well confirmed in this work should we start to introduce a sense of moving out laterally, with the inside leg applied further back. This will be discussed further in Chapters 5 and 8 but the first stage is best done on the circle. Shoulder-fore is a useful suppling movement as shown in the accompanying photograph with an older horse who had never done it before. Simply turn the upper body as you look a little more towards the centre of the circle. Then, think forwards and sideways – so the horse moves away from the pressure of your inside leg. To stay in balance, the horse is then compelled to

When the rider's leg moves out of its dropped position to nudge behind the girth, the horse will naturally want to move sideways. Balance must be kept in the shoulder-fore through a correctly turned upper body and support with the outside aids.

step deeper underneath himself – a good example of how the classical aids invite the horse to make the correct response.

At this stage, as with a normal circle, the outside leg should be fairly passive, but it must be there – to prevent the quarters from straying out – as does the outside rein. We will discuss the role of the outside aids more precisely in Chapters 5 and 6.

THINGS TO GUARD AGAINST

- Try not to move the inside leg behind the girth on the turn or circle for all normal forward work.
- Asking for lateral work too early can lead to a crooked horse who will never track up correctly on straight lines or for general figure work.
- Pushing down hard on the heel in a bend or turn may alter the feeling of weight in the seat bones, stiffen the back of the thigh and make it hard for the horse to move around your leg.

THINK POSITIVE

Always prepare the horse for every circle, turn or movement to be made by asking for the correct bend well in advance. The turn across the diagonal, for example, will be better balanced and straighter if you ensure that your horse is well supported by the inside leg before you leave the track. The turn up the centre line must be prepared in the same way.

OPPOSITE PAGE The turn across the diagonal show:
1. The preparation – sit up, half-halt, inside leg asking for bend.
2. Slight opening of the inside rein, more pressure on the ball of the inside foot taking weight right.
3. Turning of upper body and inside foot pointing in required direction, as outside leg applies pressure on horse's body.
4. Straightening onto the diagonal line through the channel of all the aids.

CLASSICAL QUOTES

'Delicacy is the use of the hands.... A hand should be firm but delicate. That hand which by giving and taking properly, gains its point with the least force, is the best.'

— EARL OF PEMBROKE, ENGLISH SCHOOL

✦

'We must be careful when making the horse straight not to bend it in front of the withers. We must not loosen the muscles in front of the withers for we need to build them up on either side of the neck so it is steady in front of the withers.'

— KLIMKE, GERMAN SCHOOL

✦

'The way to teach a totally untrained horse to change direction is to use the opening rein. In the beginning the outside hand should be totally passive.'

— VAN SCHAIK, DUTCH SCHOOL

✦

'All horses loosen up quickly if they are flexed. It is a fact that all horses by nature go more or less flexed to one side, either to the left or to the right but never perfectly straight.'

— MÜSELER, GERMAN SCHOOL

✦

'The mistake most people make when trying to straighten the horse is to push the hindquarters out, when what you should do is bring the shoulders in.'

— HESTER, ENGLISH SCHOOL

'Used perpendicularly to the horse's body, pressure of the right leg will cause it to flex and become concave on the right side.'

— DECARPENTRY, SCHOOL OF SAUMUR

✦

'When riding, the more the rider pushes [against the horse] with the inside leg on the girth to tilt the ribcage, the less hand will be needed to request an inside bend through the turns and circles.'

— BLIGNAULT, SOUTH AFRICAN SCHOOL

✦

'It is with the legs that one imparts lateral inflexion to the horse's body. A horse that refuses to inflex his body in obedience to the aids can resist and evade all our commands.'

— BURGER, GERMAN SCHOOL

✦

'The vibration, a quivering of the fingers on the reins ... must be executed without appreciably moving the hand or the wrist and must be skilfully graded. It is the perfection of touch that produces the "insinuating hand".'

— DECARPENTRY, SCHOOL OF SAUMUR

5

THE ROLE OF
THE OUTSIDE REIN

Engagement and Co-ordination

ENGAGEMENT – THE VITAL factor in developing efficient and graceful gaits – cannot occur until the horse feels a sense of *connection* from his hind legs to the forehand. In the early days of training, this connection – normal to the horse in freedom and the main factor in promoting athletic movement – is broken. The weight of the rider is, after all, a considerable load to bear.

To reconnect the flow of energy from the driving hind legs to the forehand, the horse will require a gradual readjustment of his balance to enable him to produce greater power behind. The use of good transitions and suppling exercises designed for this purpose will require rather more than a wish and a prayer. It is time to venture into the realms of academic riding, since good theory will help the physical requirements and save a lot of time, once we understand its main principles.

THE WHOLE HORSE

This is where our knowledge about the outside rein becomes so very important. In simple language, the use of the outside rein not only controls the horse's shoulders; its influence extends right back to the hindquarters, the powerhouse for the whole horse/rider unit.

In Chapter 4, we discussed lateral flexion and how to request it. Bend requires the horse's body to shorten to the inside as both ends gently curve in. This simply cannot happen unless the horse can stretch to the outside. Obviously, the

ABOVE Riding from the inside leg to the outside rein is one of the oldest precepts of school riding. A well-schooled horse will flex from the inside leg alone, but the bend must always be supported from the outside if the horse is not to 'jack-knife' with a loss of balance.

LEFT For the novice horse, the framing effect of both reins is very important and the outside rein should be sufficiently giving for the horse to stretch into it on circles and turns, as clearly shown here.

'longer' outside half of his body will fill the outside rein of its own accord. It is the rider's job to allow this to happen and, indeed, to accommodate it.

INSIDE LEG TO OUTSIDE HAND

The concept of riding 'inside leg to outside rein' is nothing new. It is a very good one if correctly understood. Unfortunately, it has become something of a catchphrase and has led to riders fussing with their legs and tightening the outside rein. This is a very different feel from maintaining inside bend with a quiet, supportive inside leg and a constant but elastic contact to the outside.

Too much pressure on the outside rein will block the freedom of the outside shoulder to come around in a circle or turn. Horses who lead with the croup or tilt the head are typical of this very common fault. Instead the rider must *allow* a little more through the outside hand (elbow or shoulder) in every turn or bend. Nevertheless, there comes a point when the outside hand says 'far enough'. At this point, it can resist passively.

It is vital that the rein aids, like those of the leg, are subtle and complement each other – one asks as one allows – and the roles may reverse from moment to moment. The only time the schooled horse will look as though he is stretched equally into both reins is out hacking, coming down the centre

line or crossing the diagonal. Even then, a diligent rider will begin to prepare in good time for the next bend by asking for gentle inside flexion, well before reaching the point of departure.

A good way of testing your understanding of contact is to ride serpentines where you will be constantly aware of these changes. Remember, most horses find it harder to bend on one particular rein, but if we can assist the stretch to the outside, this will improve.

THINK 'INSIDE OUT'

Nowadays, when so many riders rely on a direct rein aid – usually to the inside – for almost every manoeuvre, it can be quite a challenge to teach the directional roles of the outside rein. If we are on the right rein in the middle of the school

OPPOSITE PAGE AND ABOVE In every movement requiring inside bend the horse will clearly stretch to the outside. Ensure your outside shoulder follows the horse round in the turn and ease the rein sufficiently through the outside elbow and fingers. The more the bend, the greater the stretch so at times the horse should fill the rein.

Here, the young horse is nudged out to the track by Lucy's inside leg. Her outside hand has clearly opened to 'receive' the horse, whilst the inside rein is relatively passive.

and want to move out to the track to our left, pulling on the left (outside) rein will only bend the horse the wrong way and the quarters will fall in.

Instead, the horse must first be requested to flex right and, once this is achieved, the pressure of the inside (right) leg at the girth pushes the horse out to the track and into a receiving left rein. In this way the outside rein takes on an opening role, whilst the inside hand maintains bend and moves against the neck. The same (indirect) action[1] of the inside hand can be used to enlarge the circle while the inside leg continues to apply pressure at the girth.

OPPOSITE EFFECT

To bring the circle in again, the outside rein must now act in a 'closing' way – i.e. against the neck, as the inside rein asks or opens. It is very important that as one rein opens its opposite number supports or closes – except as explained – on straight lines when everything equalises again.

---

1 The indirect action of the inside rein will be discussed more fully in Chapter 8.

INDIRECT REIN

The term 'indirect rein' simply means that we are requesting the horse to move in the opposite direction. It can be used both with the inside and outside rein although, in this chapter, we are most concerned with the latter.

The feel and implementation of this important rein aid is not dissimilar to the idea of neck-reining in Western riding, but it is important never to allow it to cross over the horse's neck, or we simply negate its action.

Turning in a balanced way, i.e. on the hocks, is one of the first exercises with which to explore its benefits. The rider must first invite inside flexion – see Chapter 4 – but that is virtually all the inside rein has to do! At this point, the outside rein and leg take over to ensure a smooth turn off the track by

To reduce the circle or spiral it down, my outside rein has closed against Q's neck and is used here as an indirect rein aid. The outside leg mirrors the action of the outside hand.

In the turn on the hocks, the outside left rein has a more important role to play than the inside. Closing against the neck, it guides the forehand in the opposite direction while the hindlegs engage to mark time behind.

moving or closing against the base of the neck. 'Think of the outside wall closing in on you so the whole horse moves away from it – never pull him round by the head!' is my maxim for novice riders.

NARROWING THE GAP

For some, this more refined use of the reins can be revolutionary. Think of a corridor – provided by hands and legs – but make sure it's a friendly place to go! As the horse becomes more educated, the hands may move closer together for collection, so both reins will lightly clad the horse's neck. Once the student

The reins should provide a 'funnel' for the horse's energy as it passes up and over the horse's back – whatever the gait – so that there is no restriction in the horse's neck.

appreciates the importance of keeping the hands rigorously opposite each other, the corridor can then be moved gently to right or left.

It now makes sense to bring *both* hands slightly right to turn right; *both* hands slightly left to turn left. This action automatically opens the inside rein and brings its opposite number to bear against the withers so the indirect aid of the outside hand becomes automatic. The horse can now turn and change direction seamlessly and naturally and riding takes on a whole new dimension.

DISCONNECTION

Of course, pulling the horse's head round with an isolated rein 'aid' should never enter the picture since it separates the neck from the rest of the horse's body. Horses are very willing but the more we steer them like a bicycle, the more we overburden the forelegs and deny them their ability to push from behind. Second, without understanding how to reconnect the hindquarters or engage the 'engine' with the correct use of both legs and both reins, we will never achieve a balanced ride, or indeed a horse who is built to last.

LATERAL WORK AND BEYOND

Progressing up the Scales of Training, we might now be forgiven for thinking that the indirect rein aids take over the majority of our work. The truth is, there is an almost continuous interplay between the direct and indirect aids, governed by the rider's sense of balance and feel.

In the shoulder-in, inside flexion may first be confirmed on the circle with a direct inside rein aid, but it is the outside rein which controls the degree of bend and helps support the angle of the forehand as it moves off the track.

Shoulder-in is the only exercise when the rider's inside leg may apply pressure just behind the centre of gravity to persuade the hind legs to step sideways. Think of your outside hand *receiving* the horse's energy.

With a novice horse reluctant to move up the track it may help momentarily to open the outside hand, inviting the outside shoulder to move that way.

This fifteen-year-old happy hacker has never done a day's dressage in his life, yet here he is at a public demo, taking his first lateral steps into a feeling outside rein that guides him up the track.

THE POWER OF TOUCH

An indirect outside rein aid is also invaluable in movements such as travers, half-pass, canter pirouette and so on. The horse should already be moving into and around the rider's inside leg while the outside rein supports the bend and dictates how far. Horses have little difficulty in recognising this aid and often the weight of the rein against the neck is sufficient. A touch of our knuckles is also most effective. Thus we indicate 'sideways' to the whole forehand and again these effects extend all the way back to the hindquarters.

In the canter half-pass, the weight of my right rein against Prazer's neck acts indirectly to send him left. A gentle check, and a momentary opening (away from the wither) reminds the outside hind not to stray.

ONE-HANDED

When riding with one hand (see Chapter 12) the outside rein will naturally rest against the horse's neck as the inside rein yields to right or left, so nothing that is learned at this level will have to be re-taught at the higher levels.

The proof of correct riding should always be clear to see. When both hands appear to do nothing, when the rider's body mirrors that of the horse – shoulders to shoulders, hips to hips, hands together, we are on the right track.

In one-handed riding, both reins take the horse to the right, both reins to the left. In this half-pirouette in walk, the left rein acts indirectly against the neck, while the right reins soften to receive.

REINS OF SILK

As the horse becomes more supple, both the inside and outside rein may soften gently, even loop, though rarely at the same time. This is not because the rider has relinquished the contact. On the contrary, it is generally because – in that moment – the horse no longer relies on it for balance. This is a sign of fine equitation and a finely tuned, obedient and engaged horse.

In Chapter 6 we shall be examining a further role of the outside rein – the application of half-halts, which will particularly help in the canter work.

THINGS TO GUARD AGAINST

Riding out to the track or into the corners may be seriously compromised if the outside rein bears against the horse's neck. In walk and trot it may prevent the hind legs from tracking up correctly and in canter it may result in the quarters drifting in. No one has difficulty with opening the inside rein, but it is too easy to forget that the outside can be opened too.

THINK POSITIVE

Keep watching your horse to make sure he is correctly inflexed to right or left. Soften your jaw to the same side – the horse will feel it. When you approach the track, ride from inside leg to outside hand – as on a circle. When leaving the track, think of the rein aids for turn on the hocks, whatever gait you are in.

CLASSICAL QUOTES

'If your horse tries to cut in towards the inside of the circle, open your outside rein and support with your inside leg.'

— KOTTAS, SCHOOL OF VIENNA

✦

'By pulling with the inside hand, with the opposition of the outside hand, one prevents engagement of the inside hind.'

— BURGER, GERMAN SCHOOL

✦

'To straighten a horse we should act on his forehand not on his hindquarters. If the haunches are carried to the left, a right indirect rein will straighten him by putting his shoulders in line.'

— BEUDANT, SCHOOL OF SAUMUR

✦

'The rider must maintain a certain tension on the outside rein and in the later stages of training, it is entirely with the outside rein that the rider determines the degree of lateral flexion of the poll.'

— BURGER, GERMAN SCHOOL

✦

'The inside rein leads the horse into the circle and the outside rein is responsible for the correct position and the gradually decreased size of the circle.'

— PODHAJSKY, SCHOOL OF VIENNA

✦

'The correct inside bend is evident by the slight loop or soft inside rein and the straight outside rein.'

— BLIGNAULT, SOUTH AFRICAN SCHOOL

'The lengthening of the indirect rein, to cause flexion to the opposite side, is its primary effect. It can be used on any horse.... Provided only that there exists a fair acceptance of the bridle.'

— WYNMALEN, DUTCH SCHOOL

✦

'Though criticised by some, the neck rein has a definite advantage over any other rein effect in that it acts on the neck, not on the mouth. You can carry it out, if necessary, on loose reins.'

— FROISSARD, FRENCH SCHOOL

✦

'In the shoulder-in, the inside leg must accentuate its forward action, to promote the displacement of the mass in the direction of the outside shoulder and the outside rein must likewise "lead" the forehand along the track.'

— DECARPENTRY, SCHOOL OF SAUMUR

THE ROLE OF
THE OUTSIDE LEG

Engagement and Canter Transitions

İN VERY SIMPLE TERMS the role of the rider's legs could be described as follows: *'Inside leg takes care of the forehand; outside leg controls the quarters'*.

This is not a bad maxim to instil awareness of the different leg aids, especially the need to separate both position and action for each effect. All this requires discipline but it should lead to a time when we only have to think what we want for the horse to understand. Horses have incredible memories.

FEEL AND TACT

Having described the forward 'driving' influence of the rider's legs applied together, as well as the bending action of the inside leg applied at the girth, the time has come to look at the different roles of the outside leg. In the higher-level exercises, we soon discover that, as with the reins, the legs likewise will need to aid independently of each other. Just as we spoke of hands without legs and legs without hands, so there must be a nano-second in between, say, the bending action of one leg and the receiving or supporting action of the other.

To understand all this better, we must try to appreciate what the horse *feels*. There is a big difference between a) moving into pressure – to step under – and b) moving away from pressure – to step sideways. In dressage, we often have to apply these different weight aids all in the same movement, almost in the same moment. It can be quite a juggling act and it helps to know *when* and *how* and *for what purpose*.

Without the correct theory, it is very easy to confuse the horse. Much 'naughty' or unwarranted behaviour stems from the rider applying all the aids at once. Few realise just how powerful the interaction of the rider's leg can be, especially on a hot-blooded horse like a Thoroughbred, Arab or Iberian. Unless we use tact and timing, it is all too easy for the horse to feel trapped, which can only lead to resistance or a desire to break out.

For an eye-opener on the leg aids and their effects, riding a higher-level schoolmaster is an enlightening experience. Such a horse will immediately tell the student when they have given the 'wrong' cue. Noting each response leads to a better sense of *feel*. Often, the rider's muscle memory has to be redirected. Eventually, 'aids' which were thought to be correct are replaced by ones which actually work and, through positive reinforcement, the work is transformed.

ABOVE, LEFT By directing a little more pressure into my right seatbone (stirrup), Prazer very naturally bends and moves that way.

ABOVE, RIGHT In the shoulder-in, I first ask for bend by sitting to the inside, then to progress down the track, may slightly deepen the out-side (seatbone) stirrup.

BENDS AND CIRCLES

Just as the rider's inside leg helps to stimulate the forehand – e.g. bend, impulsion, lift, etc. – so the outside leg has its own role to play. Placed behind the girth it should *guard, guide or energise the quarters* in all three gaits.

On a circle for example, some horses may avoid working behind by 'throwing' the quarters out. The rider's inside leg slipping back is one cause, but a lack of support to the outside is equally bad. The mere presence of the outside leg reaching behind the girth to guide the quarters on a circular track can transform the movement.

Ultimately, we are looking to encourage greater engagement in both hind legs. The outside hind is too often forgotten and the main purpose of the rider's outside leg is to keep it pushing under.

The smaller the circle the more the horse has to bend or engage the quarters and push from behind. The rider must sit tall with a supple back to alleviate the load, and here, my outside hip opens to free up the leg aid.

SHOULDER-IN

We have already discussed our first few lateral steps on the circle, generally known as shoulder-fore. The shoulder-in proper has always been deemed the key to collection and will be discussed further in Chapter 8. As regards the outside leg, this aid is often neglected and yet it is arguably the most important, since it supports the angle of the movement in relation to the track. Whilst the lower leg talks to the hind-end, the role of the outside hip and thigh to guide and contain the forehand is a subtle, but nevertheless important one. Together with the influence of the outside rein, this can make all the difference in determining whether we want to proceed on three or four tracks.[1] As for the lower part of the leg, this is responsible for keeping the outside hind engaged and energetic. Without this aid, it is all too easy for the quarters to escape and for the horse to become 'disconnected'. In the shoulder-in, the influence of the rider's inside leg is very powerful but the work can only be correct when counterbalanced by the outside rein and the outside leg.

---

[1] Since the standard form of shoulder-in required in competition is on three tracks, some readers may be unaware that the exercise can legitimately be performed on four tracks, provided the horse is sufficiently supple to do so in a correct manner.

Here we see the importance of the outside knee and thigh to support the angle of the shoulder-in. Note the active inside hind as it adducts, stepping forward and through.

TRAVERS AND HALF-PASS

In travers and half-pass, the roles of the rider's legs are reversed from those of shoulder-in. Instead of the outside leg supporting the movement and preventing the hindquarters from escaping outwards, it now nudges them sideways in the opposite direction to step under and engage. Instead of the inside leg asking the horse to move away from pressure, it invites the horse to move into it. We tend to think of the inside leg alone promoting bend, but for these lateral movements, try thinking 'outside in'. Allow your outside leg – applied just behind the girth – to place your horse *around* your inside leg, which remains quiet and pillar-like at the girth. The engagement will be far superior.

Dropping weight into the inside stirrup takes pressure off the horse's body. The horse now feels he has room to move into it. This concept is well understood in Natural Horsemanship but not generally taught in dressage today. Yet all we are doing – yet again – is using gravity to show the horse the way. Once again, this *allows* the horse to follow us – which again leads to positive reinforcement.

In travers or quarters-in on the circle, the outside leg and outside rein guide the horse laterally, while my weight is directed to the inside – keeping the horse bending that way.

CANTER AIDS

The canter aid depends on the rider's legs taking a similar position to the turns on the hocks or half-pass. Gently weighting the inside stirrup lightens the outside seat bone and facilitates the canter depart. Generally, and particularly with young horses, it is the outside leg which is the most effective at requesting the canter depart which starts in the outside hind.

With the young horse, always start from a circle or corner and ride straight down the track. Straighten the horse's neck, just prior to asking with the outside leg. This will free the inside shoulder and assist the strike-off. Sitting lightly may help with horses who are overly keen. Too many riders push with the seat for the canter depart, which may simply makes the horse trot faster or, when canter is achieved, tip the balance onto the forehand.

For horses who tend to rush, a degree of collection will help and some horses may find it easier to canter from walk than from trot. A gentle half-halt on the outside rein, helps shift weight to the hocks with the cue that something is about to happen. The leg aids are then applied immediately and the moment the horse responds, the fingers release.

Again, it is the *feel* of the leg and seat aids that provides a good outcome. If the rider's outside hip is tight, the aid applied behind the girth is likely to be

BELOW, LEFT There can be no canter without the push-off from the outside hind. It is a grave mistake to sit down hard and drive with the seat. Instead, lighten the outside seatbone to facilitate the canter depart.

BELOW, RIGHT However correct your outside aids, the horse greatly relies on the support of your inside leg at the girth to keep the canter balanced.

From a lighter seat, we can develop the full seat once the horse is established in the gait. Either way, we must continue to sit up and look between the ears at all times.

from the calf only, and the horse will find it harder to respond. It is important that the rider's outside leg moves back from a supple hip – but it should not move back too far.

Similarly, if the inside leg is not placed correctly at the girth with a feeling of 'leading' the horse into canter, he may simply ignore the request. Once canter is established, the inside leg may then, and only then 'ask' for more bend, more lift, etc., but be careful not to muddle the horse by asking for everything at once.

BALANCE IN CANTER

Since cantering in the school can be quite demanding for a young horse, it is often better to ride 20m half-circles before requesting full ones. Later, we will progress to spiralling in on circles, turns or loops. At all times our balance must be impeccable – whether in the full or light seat. Always think of riding 'out' to the circle, 'out' to the track and open the outside rein to assist if necessary. If the horse has a tendency to 'motorbike', it may help to transfer weight momentarily into the outside stirrup.

As the horse becomes more confident and collected, we may request the canter with the inside leg alone. We have already discussed the stepping down effect into the inside stirrup. A quick press with the inside shin at the sensitive girth area will give lift to the canter, before allowing the leg to drop again. If the horse has a tendency to lean, the inside leg should apply short, light touches to encourage better bend and lighten the forehand.

On corners, circles and turns, riders must resist leaning in themselves. Growing tall – even imagining an extra rib to the inside of your body – can do wonders. Balance is also helped by the application of gentle half-halts on the outside rein, but never at the expense of blocking the horse's outside shoulder as it comes around.

There may be moments when the horse will try to lean or take hold. Resist imbalance by growing an 'extra' rib to the inside and putting more weight into the outside stirrup.

COUNTER-CANTER

Provided we use exactly the same leg and weight aids as we did in true canter, the progression to counter-canter is no big deal. The horse does not mind which way round the school he is travelling if we make it easy for him by starting on a loop, moving later to big half-circles, then gradually easing him back to the track on the new rein. Building up trust in this way allows him to concentrate on the feel of the rider rather than worrying about which rein he is on. The important thing is to keep the original inside bend (now to the outside of the school) look over the original leading leg, keep your weight on the original inside seat bone and lighten the outside seat bone (now to the inside of the school).

Many riders automatically change their head position as they arrive on the track in counter-canter but this, in itself, can cause the horse to change legs or disunite. Provided all the original canter aids remain in place, there should be no reason for the horse to change legs. Such consistency will pay off when,

Here, I have just asked for counter-canter on the right rein. My right leg has moved back to engage Prazer's right hind for the strike-off, and my weight, gaze and energy is all to the left.

later in the horse's training, we can ask for counter-canter out of true canter with a flying change. Again, if the aids have been clear and correct throughout, the horse should understand (see Chapter 10).

CANTER HALF-PASS

For canter half-pass, or simply moving the horse off the track to make a loop or turn, the rider's weight will remain to the inside – as in normal canter – but it will be the influence of the *outside* rein and *outside* leg which sends the horse in a lateral direction. The pressure of the outside leg behind the girth will now intensify. There is no need to bring it further back than normal. This is a classic case of 'weight against' and – with the benefit of speed – the horse naturally

The three tracks of canter half-pass are plain to see. My weight is in my right stirrup, while my (unseen) left leg sends us laterally forward. Ideally, there could be more bend – hence my spur just touching the bend 'button' at the girth.

Canter half-pass on the same rein from another angle. Ideally my outside leg should be doing less and I have dropped my inside shoulder instead of staying square.

moves away from the pressure. This aid must be used with discretion if the quarters are not to lead ahead of the forehand. It must also be counterbalanced by the inside leg acting at the girth to support the bend, to limit the sideways progression and to keep the horse forward thinking.

OUR SECRET AIDS

Many good riders are quite unconscious of how much they use the knee and thigh for both bend and direction. Since these aids are largely invisible, they are rarely mentioned in a riding lesson. Yet from a safety point of view the rider's feet, knees and hips must always look forward never outward. In this way they lightly frame the horse's body and can give extra support when necessary. With a higher-level horse, the press of a knee is often sufficient to nudge him into the desired direction.

THINGS TO GUARD AGAINST

Tightness in the rider's hips has a deleterious effect on the framing influence of the legs and the application of clear, distinct aids. Before settling into the saddle, always open each hip independently and allow each leg to drop into place. Knees that gape open provide an escape route for the horse's energy. Never blame the horse if he offers the wrong leg in the canter depart – first look to yourself.

THINK POSITIVE

Encouragement with the voice is often helpful. The rhythm of the word – 'Can-ter!' – can be a good cue in the early days. Praise when the horse gets it right and, as the work becomes more balanced, reward him by intermittently giving with the inside rein. This is a good proof that he is sufficiently flexed over the inside, leading leg.

CLASSICAL QUOTES

'Used singly, one leg produces effects which vary according to the manner and the place of application.'

— DECARPENTRY, SCHOOL OF SAUMUR

✦

'To indicate the canter, if the rider gives the aid of his [outside] right leg at the precise moment when the right hind is about to swing forward, the horse can start the canter immediately with the right lead.'

— BURGER, GERMAN SCHOOL

✦

'On the opposite side to the concave flexion, the outside leg automatically finds it place somewhat further behind the girth... . Back there, it is able to act as a restraining and driving agent if the croup turns out.'

— SEUNIG, GERMAN SCHOOL

✦

'The outside leg placed passively behind the girth gives the signal for the canter and prevents the horse from carrying his hindquarters to the outside, while the inside leg, pushing forward on the girth, makes the horse strike off.'

— PODHAJSKY, SCHOOL OF VIENNA

✦

'Demand a regular placement of the horse at the canter, which consists of a slight bend to the side of the leg on which he is cantering. This bend is important for later on it will become an indication for the horse to take a canter depart as well as to change leads.'

— JOUSSEAUME, SCHOOL OF SAUMUR

'The aids of the thighs and hams are produced by pressing them together to move the horse forwards or by pressing only the thigh or ham of the outside to cause the horse to move towards the inside.'

— LA GUÉRINIÈRE, SCHOOL OF VERSAILLES

'The rider in all these half pass exercises must be sure that his body does not lean to the outside or inside; the rider's weight must remain in the centre of the horse. To avoid the body leaning to the outside, sit down on the inside seat bone.'

— OLIVEIRA, PORTUGUESE SCHOOL

THE WEIGHT AIDS OF THE SEAT

Collection, Halt, Half-halt and Rein-back

WITH THE YOUNG OR novice horse, our main preoccupation has been to allow him to go forward within the gentle framework of our hands and legs. Transitions require the interaction of the whole body, the legs playing a bigger part than the hands. The take and give of the fingers for an upward or downward transition is generally accompanied by the take and give of the rider's legs, seat and upper body which influence the whole – although not necessarily in the same moment.

As the horse matures, we should become more aware of the effects of our upper body and how it affects the seat. As with the aids of hand and leg, the seat can either take or give. The 'take' of course refers to collection. If more lessons for the higher-level student were devoted to the seat aids, we might see much kinder hands and there would be less inclination to shorten horses through the neck in order to remain in control.

So what exactly to do we mean by the take and give of the rider's seat? First, let us clarify that this has absolutely nothing to do with pushing, which may well hollow the horse's spine. On the contrary, the seat aids should be subtle and almost invisible since they rely on the tone and elasticity of the rider's abdominal, back and adductor muscles which are not so easily observed.

Second, no seat aid can be given with real precision unless the rider sits *still!* This may sound like a contradiction but, as with the hands and legs, unless we are quiet to start with, the horse will not notice when an aid is given. It is also

The three-point seat where the rider is in contact with the saddle from back to front (two seat-bones and crotch) is generally accepted as the most balanced for the sensitivities of good dressage as well as safety. It places us vertically over the horse's strongest point so we can ease or deepen the weight at will.

vital we sit as close as possible over the horse's centre of gravity, i.e. up to the pommel (waist to hands) with the seat bones resting in the centre of the saddle.

UP THE BODY

The rider's body acts on that of a horse rather like a bridge. The bridge must, of course, allow energy to pass through and under. For this reason it requires a supportive structure and firm foundations. Vertical and well-rooted, gravity keeps it in place but, in relation to the horse, this can only work when the rider sits up with supple loins and learns to let go with the legs.

From open hip joints and relaxed legs, you are more able to stimulate the horse sufficiently to produce and gather the energy required in collection. Ask

The more you sit up, the firmer you feel. Good posture must never be confused with stiffness. Opening your 'frontline', i.e. the abdominals, keeps your back flexible and supported, better able to absorb movement.

at the girth with light, swift touches of the lower leg to bring the horse's back up and think of sitting up and remaining *above* it all. Never ever push down; instead allow gravity to keep you in place.

From now on, everything we do with the upper body and legs will change the feel and the pressures of our seat on the horse's back. The 'bridge' will collapse if the abdominal muscles are slack; by firming up with the shoulders, back and sternum and with the navel to the fore, you can control this stored energy at will. 'Up the body, down the weight!' is the maxim at Vienna.

DOWN THE WEIGHT

To stay in balance, the entire underside of the pelvis from front to back must contact the saddle. A good saddle, rising at the twist to support the crotch, will direct the rider's weight to its lowest point through the seat bones (i.e. a good hand's breadth from the cantle) and as close as possible to the horse's centre of balance. This all-embracing contact of the rider's seat promotes a quiet, elegant and upright position which allows for subtle changes. It has come to be known as the three-point seat, with numerous references in both ancient and modern classical books, and it is practised at the great riding academies of the world

Once the seat is secure, there is no need to grip with the thighs, knees or lower leg. Their sheer weight places them in the perfect position for whatever is required next.

The taller we sit, the greater the downward pull of the legs. The stretch should be through the front of our thighs, into our knees and thence to the ground. This keeps our seat central, making it easy to 'let go' with our legs – so important for the gathering or collection of the horse as we advance his education. The feeling is not unlike that of riding without stirrups. Once we tune into gravity, the sheer *weight* of the leg falling away keeps us rooted. We should never worry about losing our stirrups again.

OPENING AND CLOSING

Whilst the seat should remain more-or-less neutral for riding the young horse forward or for hacking, dressage proper requires greater awareness. How we use our seat should never be forced or contrived, but every change of balance

and gait will rely on subtle changes within ourselves. With practice, these fine aids should develop naturally, since every movement we make on the ground is based on similar principles.

In simple terms, the pelvis acts rather like a gearbox. In riding, its position – our seat – can regulate just how much energy we retain or let through. For example, in bringing our shoulders fractionally behind the vertical, the pelvis 'opens', allowing more energy to be released from the hindquarters to the forehand. As we shall see in Chapter 9, when correctly done and assisted with appropriate leg aids, we now have an effective driving aid. This is, of course, the opposite of how we use the seat for collection.

By contrast, when we sit in the vertical, knees down, legs back a little, the pelvis is more closed in front. This complements the bringing together of the horse's energy – the word 'collection' being very appropriate. Tilting the balance to the front of the saddle allows the horse to flex his back, step deep underneath and produce shorter, more elevated steps. The more we draw up, the more we take his energy up with us. This, in turn, brings control, cadence and balance to the gaits.

As already discussed, moving the legs too much behind the vertical may put on the 'handbrake'. This works very nicely for rein-back as we relieve pressure from the back of the saddle, but we must always release, sit up and return to

1. 'Opening the door' – allows the horse to flow forward and through you.
2. 'Door half-open' – draws the horse more under you. These feelings emanate from a good seat, core support and appropriately learning to use your centre of gravity. Invisible aids!

Closing the door in front but opening it behind is the feel we need for rein-back. Bring the chest slightly forward and the legs back. Gently close behind the girth followed by an immediate release for each and every step. The hands do very little.

neutral the moment we want to go forward again. All these nuances work together to produce a fine balancing act, but take care never to overdo things. The seat aids should be virtually invisible to anyone watching.

HIGHER AND HIGHER

Later in the horse's training (and always subtly counterbalanced by the raising of the rider's centre of gravity), a further redirection of the horse's energy can lead us to the High School airs discussed in Chapter 11. Freeing up the horse's loins facilitates the piaffe and passage – when the impulsion is held in a state of bubbling suspension – and all this will be an evolving process. We must never rush collection. 'Contained' energy transforms itself into beautiful movements in its own time and according to the strength and the ability of the horse. Having said that, often the most collected movements are offered quite spontaneously by a fit and generous horse.

CHECKLIST

At this stage of riding it is important always to have a mental picture of your entire body and how it impacts on the horse's back. Make no mistake, despite the latest numnah, the stuffing and padding of a beautifully crafted saddle, every move we make is felt.

Disciplining oneself should translate into feeling what the horse is feeling. We have to listen as well as act. Any form of tension or imbalance should be relayed back through the seat of the pants. We learn to make small but meaningful changes of weight, always returning to neutral in between.

Personally, I tend to 'look down' on myself when I ride. Others prefer a series of checks: 'Am I sitting square? Am I vertical? Have I kept my navel and sternum forward? Has my inside hip maintained position? Has my outside hip opened sufficiently? Are my knees sufficiently deep? Is my neck at the back of my collar? Are my fingers and ankles relaxed?' All these, practised on a daily basis, are very useful.

HALT

Of course, many riders use the seat aids without ever thinking about it. They may never have had a lesson in their life, but by conditioning themselves and their horse to what works, they develop the feel for opening or closing the

ABOVE LEFT Once we have impulsion, bringing our legs back diverts the energy upward as well as forward to give us the lift needed for passage. Again, the upper body must be proud with a high centre of gravity to draw the horse up.

ABOVE RIGHT For a balanced halt, think up rather than bearing down, with both legs behind the girth. Note my hand indicating my centre of gravity.

door. Good riders will scarcely use the rein for halt since the combined aid of seat, legs and upper body does it much better. Their downward transitions will be smooth and seamless.

Bad riders think impulsion can only be stopped at the horse's mouth – by which time it has generally gone too far. They have no comprehension of controlling it from the centre and have to rely on stronger bits and harsher aids, which invariably hollow the horse. As Baucher famously wrote: *'I like the horse to be behind the hand and in front of the legs, so that the centre of gravity is placed between these two aids, as it is only on this condition that the horse is absolutely under the control of the rider.'*

COLLECTION FIRST

Clearly, the more we are able to develop the weight aids, the better our riding. For me, collection has to come before extension, since without the gathering of energy there can be no serious releasing or lengthening.

It should go without saying that the more we wish to collect the horse, the more we need impulsion. To start, it may require something of a juggling act to preserve the flow of energy from the hind legs and to collect or keep it at the ready for the next movement, be it sideways, upwards, backwards or simply more forwards. No one can teach you how to do this, but riding a fully trained and collected horse can at least give you the feel, so you can gradually develop it for yourself.

To half-halt correctly, sit central and support your diaphragm. Then draw up, square your elbows and simply squeeze the fingers of one or both hands. Then soften forward again.

HALF-HALT

It is not just in riding that we learn to harness energy. Most athletes, and particularly dancers, ice skaters and gymnasts, know when to keep it in reserve – to hold or fix with their bodies – and when and how to allow it out – sometimes in a great surge! And, of course, all this has nothing to do with the hands!

The half-halt can be like this. Remember this is not a full transition, but the feeling could be described as preparing for a transition. It should be a momentary instruction – a second's check or fix – prior to sending forward or re-channelling the impulsion for whatever is required next.

Try not to lean back in the half-halt. Rather sit up with shoulders back! A consequence of the half-halt will be a reduction in the length of stride, but we are rewarded with higher, lighter steps. In the early days, do not be greedy with these or you will end up with choppy gaits. As with everything in riding, we must work the horse both ways – forward and more together – to develop his strength and understanding. It's a very gradual process.

HOW?

Unfortunately, many people think the half-halt is only to do with the hands. Many draw the hand back, which only invites resistance. Try instead to think of half-halting through your core as you close the fingers. This will be felt down the length of the rein and if this is not sufficient, then raise the hand gently, but only an inch or so. As you do so, breathe, draw up and *hold* – through the small of the back. Let the breath out when the horse obeys and your hand will automatically give again.

Here, a slight tilt of the pelvis lightens my seat on the back of the saddle for a very collected canter. The horse lifts his back in response to a high centre of gravity and a momentary half-halt. Ideally, my heels should be down.

This feeling is generally transmitted all the way through the seat. A correct half-halt allows the horse to draw the hindquarters deeper under the rider's centre of gravity. In so doing, the well-schooled horse will bend his joints to greater effect and learn to 'sit'.

As with a ballerina, it is from those moments of 'hold' through the rider's core, back and pelvis that the balance is perfected – for whatever manoeuvre is requested next. In the shoulder-in, for example, I always think of a moment of fix, to allow the horse *time* to step under, to flex his joints and to take his weight back. In this movement, and in half-pass and canter strike-off, I would half-halt with the outside rein alone.

'FIX, TAKE AND GIVE'

It was Nuno Oliveira who introduced us to this perceptive little saying. Anyone who attended the Annual Conference of the Association of British Riding Schools (ABRS) in 1987 and 1988 will remember this advice being given out to every rider on every horse. If the horse is heavy on the hands and powering on rather too much, say in trot on a straight line, one would probably use both hands. The feeling is subtle. The fingers close very firmly, very quickly. With some horses, a slight rotation of the wrists might help and there should be a very slight upward influence to the action, but never at the risk of jerking. With it comes a corresponding 'hold' through the wrists, elbows and shoulder joints. The 'fix' feeling transfers right down the rider's back and if anything the seat bones should move a little forward.

The moment the horse changes his posture, the hands must give again. Once accepted and understood, half-halts will gradually be employed more and more as we progress towards full collection. They eventually become so refined that they comprise a vital part of the collection process.

WEIGHT BACK

Strength and suppleness behind comes from the judicious and repeated practice of many different manoeuvres – start and stop, straight and bend, forward and back, right and left, together and stretched. Now that we understand the main principles of the aiding process, we will be in a much better position to ride the lateral exercises accurately and with a deeper understanding – see Chapter 8. The shoulder-in is always considered the first of these, since it not only transfers weights to the haunches but, done correctly, will engage the horse's hip, stifle, hock and fetlock joints. That is the key to lightness and collection.

Shoulder-in on the circle is a great suppling movement. The horse will adduct (step deeper under himself) rather more than in normal shoulder-in and I must ensure that my outside shoulder comes around so we stay 'lined up' throughout.

EVERYTHING IS CONNECTED TO EVERYTHING

To understand the different 'feels' required to bring about collection is very personal. We have concentrated on the seat in this chapter, but remember – nothing in your body works in isolation. Every single part of you, even the way you carry your head, will have an effect on the feel of the seat in the saddle.

Collection comes from knowing how much to regulate the flow from behind, but without energy you have nothing to play with. Bringing the weight back must never restrict the horse; it simply allows us to gather him, so that the work can flow with more brilliance the moment we release. In human terms, it's similar to 'setting one back on one's heels' – a momentary pause before doing something extraordinary.

THINGS TO GUARD AGAINST

Remember, too much of any one exercise, any one mode, will tire muscles, ligaments and joints. There can be no true collection where tension or discomfort are present. Solution: introduce variety in everything you do and collection will develop as the horse becomes more elastic and fluid.

THINK POSITIVE

Look ahead at all times; if our eyes help us control our bodies on the ground, so they will on horseback. Feel for the balance and make small adjustments only as and when required. Between each and every request, remember always to return to neutral. Remember, less is more!

CLASSICAL QUOTES

'The pelvis should be upright, with weight taken on both seat bones and the pubic bone – this is known as the three-point seat. The rider should sit in the centre of the saddle with equal weight in both seat bones.'

— KOTTAS, SCHOOL OF VIENNA

❖

'He [the rider] ought to sit upright upon the twist and not upon the buttocks; though most people think they were made by nature to do this. Thus placed in the middle of the saddle, he ought to advance as much as he can, towards the pommel.'

— DUKE OF NEWCASTLE, ENGLISH SCHOOL

❖

'Neither the effects of legs or hands can compensate for the inadequacy of the seat. The potency of the seat – that is of the weight effect – as an aid is due to the fact it evokes ... the horse's instinctive reactions to physical laws.'

— ALBRECHT, SCHOOL OF VIENNA

❖

'To collect, we need to restrain and change the distribution of the (horse's) weight.'

— KLIMKE, GERMAN SCHOOL

❖

'Every horse who is in front of the hand is behind the legs, and consequently escapes control at both ends.'

— BAUCHER, FRENCH SCHOOL

'The half-halt … is performed as a measure designed to get the horse to make an effort to support its head and neck by making it understand that it cannot find any support in the rider's hand.'

— PAILLARD, SCHOOL OF SAUMUR

✦

'The half-halt … makes the contact with the mouth light; it can be repeated frequently without interrupting the pace.'

— LA GUÉRINIÈRE, SCHOOL OF VERSAILLES

✦

'When the rein back is started on demand and carried out without haste, it is a magnificent exercise which should be repeated frequently.'

— OLIVEIRA, PORTUGUESE SCHOOL

THE INDIRECT AIDS

Shoulder-in, Travers and Half-pass

B Y THIS STAGE OF riding, we should be very clear that all the rein effects must be discreet – scarcely noticeable to the onlooker. An opening or direct rein aid does not indicate that the hand always has to move away from the horse's neck except in the early days. By the time the horse is ready for serious lateral work neither hand should appear to move.

We have already discussed the early application of the outside rein against the horse's neck as an indirect aid (see Chapter 5) to turn him in the opposite direction. As he progresses up the Scales of Training, we begin to appreciate how much this will benefit the shoulder-in, the travers and the half-pass.

Always be aware that the rider's *whole* body should complement the shoulder-in. At the accepted angle (approx. 30–35 degrees) it is essential that the rider's head, upper body, hips, knees and feet should all turn *with the horse* to look into the movement. This will naturally bring the outside rein to bear passively against the horse's neck and – provided the outside knee and thigh are also in support – the horse is less likely to lose position.

INSIDE AIDS

As a classic lateral movement, the shoulder-in is unique in that the horse is asked to bend one way and move away in the opposite direction. In shoulder-in (overleaf above), the horse is first asked to look right and move his shoulders right in response to the unseen, opening (right) rein. Just as he is about to leave the track, the inside leg must now act just behind the girth to nudge

RIGHT This is a good three-track shoulder-in with Prazer nicely bent around my inside leg. The outside rein may either support the forehand or in certain cases help lead the horse up the track.

BELOW This is a more extravagant four-track shoulder-in. More angle in our own body gives more angle to the horse. Here, my inside rein acts in an indirect way and assists the engagement of the inside hind.

him laterally in the opposite direction. In other words the right leg asks him to move into the outside (left) rein, which will issue a gentle check to confirm his position and the placement of the forehand to the track.

It is very important at this stage that the rider does not pull back with the right hand and overbend the neck to the inside. Over time, the horse will learn to step deeper under his body with the inside hind, causing the inside haunch to flex and lower thus taking the weight back. Nicely framed by both reins, the horse may now work laterally along the track without losing bend, position or collection. If all is going perfectly, the inside rein will feel light, whilst the allowing outside rein feels nicely filled.

ROLE REVERSAL

It is at this point that the inside rein may now subtly change its role by gently closing against the withers. The sideways feel is very gentle and in the direction of the outside haunch. The hand may be slightly rotated or simply indicate. As an indirect rein aid,[1] the inside rein now mirrors the effect of the inside leg, but never enough to alter the position of the horse's head. It consists of little more than the weight of the rein against the neck whilst retaining soft inside flexion (glimmer of eye and flare of nostril only), whether in shoulder-in along the track or on the circle.

Correctly done, the entire flow of the movement may now be enhanced with both reins reversing roles. With the inside rein bearing gently against the forehand, the outside rein virtually becomes the 'opening' rein. In the next moment, the latter may return to its normal role – to support the asking of the inside leg. These aids are in a state of continual, interdependent and totally unobtrusive flux. As with all balancing acts, a number of factors are involved:

- the angle of the horse to the track

- the weight in the shoulders

- the amount of bend – and –

- most important, the placing of the hind legs.

To the onlooker, everything looks quiet; the reins simply frame the horse's neck.

---

1 Known as the indirect rein of opposition fifth effect – the influence is behind the withers towards the horse's opposite haunch.

Role reversal is something that is hard to describe since it happens according to what the horse is being asked to do *in the moment*. It is often used when spiralling the circle in or out. The general rule is that the indirect effect of the outside rein will bring the circle in; the indirect effect of the inside rein will take the circle out. Remember, all these rein effects are mere nuances and must co-ordinate correctly with the aids of seat and leg. They must never oppose each other and should basically constitute invisible aids.

Spiralling the circle outward with the inside leg and the indirect use of the inside rein is a good preparation for all the lateral movements.

SHOULDER-FORE ON THE CIRCLE

To refresh the horse and make a change from our work on the track, it is good to return to work on the circle or to ride shoulder-in through a corner. This actually requires far more skill to do well than producing a good shoulder-in on the track. The amount of angle requested by the rider depends very much on the level of training. As with all training, good engagement can only come about when the horse is sufficiently supple, so take time.

In teaching riders new to this movement, the biggest difficulty seems to be that of turning with the horse for more than a couple of steps. Common faults are slack thighs, unsupportive knees and, all too often, the rider's face and upper body failing to come around with the horse. In no time at all the circumference of the circle leaches in or out. When shoulder-in is performed on the track, we only need to arrange our body in the required angle *once*; on the circle, we must adjust our body *step by step*. Only by sticking to the principle of shoulders to horse's shoulders, hips to horse's hips can riders remain 'lined up'.

OPPOSITE PAGE For the shoulder-fore or shoulder-in on the circle, the first priority is to stay 'lined up' to the horse at all times. A little more weight on the inside seatbone keeps the horse circling left, while the influence of the indirect rein sends the energy in a lateral direction in each and every sequence of this gymnastic exercise.

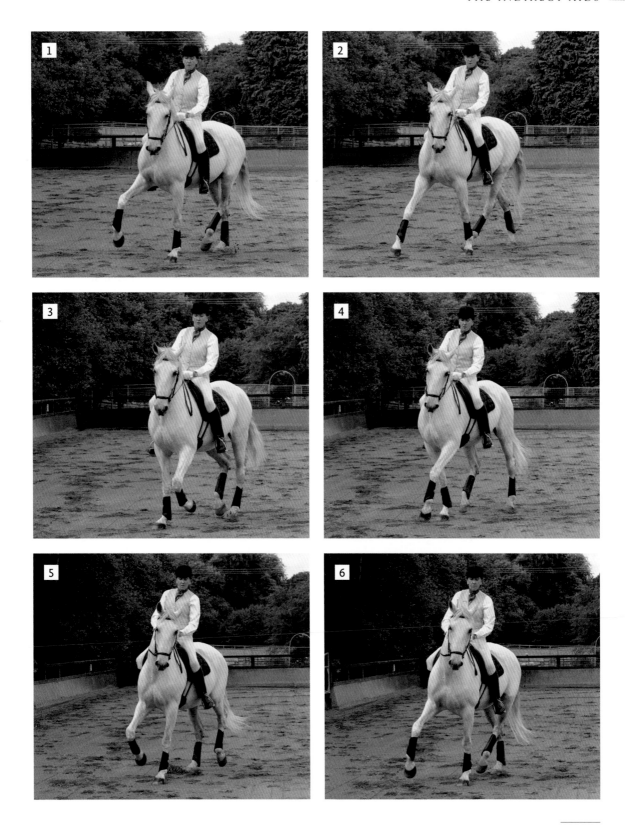

Once you have mastered these movements, everything will start to flow. Soon, the action of your lower inside leg can be replaced by just the press of the thigh. Before too long the two reins framing the horse's neck in concert with the hips and upper body will be automatic and everything will start turning nicely.

TRAVERS

As with the shoulder-in, the inside (opening) rein will request inside flexion and gently lead the horse up the track, whilst the outside rein acts indirectly against the neck. Starting from a 10m circle, the moment the horse's nose reaches the selected point (just before he completes the circle) we push him sideways along the tangent. As well as acting indirectly to indicate sideways movement, the outside rein also controls the bend and the angle of the movement.

Here too, the rider's entire body must complement that of the horse. The rider must look into the movement – at an angle to the wall – and be conscious of advancing the inside hip. In this context both the rider's hips and shoulders must be aligned to match those of the horse. The posture must be centred and firm.

The exercise of head to the wall may be ridden on three or four tracks in travers or as a half-pass. Here, the most important aid is the dropping of my weight into the inside seatbone and the angle of my hips and shoulders. The influence of the indirect (outside) rein will become apparent – see opposite – but there may be moments when the inside rein too may act indirectly to correct the placement of the shoulders to the track.

The leg aids will complement the action of the hands. The inside leg must ask intermittently at the girth for forward progression. It may also drop more weight into the inside stirrup – echoed by the inside seat bone – so the horse is encouraged to bend and move the same way.

The outside leg will apply pressure behind the girth and complement the indirect effect of the outside rein. It requests the outside hind to engage by stepping over and in front of the inside hind. The horse will now move onto three tracks. With the inside seat bone and stirrup gently weighted, the horse is persuaded to travel forward, sideways and into the movement. Later, gentle half-halts will enable us to check and control our progress down the track.

CORRECTIONS

With a horse new to travers and reticent to place himself 'head to the wall', you may wish to start the movement as part of a circle. Whilst shoulder-in can be practised regularly in this way, there is an argument that travers on the circle is not a good idea for horses who have a tendency to travel quarters-in on straight lines. On the other hand, travers on the circle is a good preparation for the canter pirouette, so again, discretion must be used.

As with the shoulder-in, the rider will need to remember to turn with the horse step by careful step throughout the process, but apart from that the normal aids prevail.

BELOW Travers or quarters-in on the circle is a good preparation for the canter pirouette. It requires more assistance from the indirect aids than is generally assumed.
1. Shows the outside rein used indirectly against the base of the neck to encourage the horse left.
2. Shows the inside rein used indirectly to keep Prazer's nose from straying off the circular track.

HALF-PASS

Exactly the same aids as those for travers will be used for half-pass. Eventually – both in walk and trot – we are looking for good crossing with both fore and hind legs, the gymnasticity of which needs to be built up gradually. Be happy with very little to start with and always give the rein forward at the slightest sign of confusion or resistance.

In the half-pass, the rider will become increasingly aware of the efficacy of the indirect (outside) rein, remembering always that all the aids must work in concert one with the other. In the half-pass, we are asking the horse to move into pressure (inside leg and inside seat bone) and away from pressure (outside leg and indirect rein). It can be quite a juggling act to harmonise all the aids whilst maintain good forward impulsion. In the early days, we should ask only for a few sideways steps at a time before riding straight forward again. Use the whole school to do this – the more open space ahead, the more encouraging for the horse.

Once the horse is able to offer half a dozen or so good steps, try riding from the centre line back to the track (or vice versa) but don't overturn the body. Your head should be flexed in the direction of travel; your eyes may slide

BELOW The indirect rein plays an important part in the positioning of the forehand in the half-pass. Here in walk, it helps prepare the horse whilst its influence extends all the way back to the outside hind. Despite weight to inside, note how my buttons remain lined up to the mane throughout.

There is so much to think about in half-pass, imagine what it is like for the horse! At the first sign of tension, be quick to release the rein and ride forward straight or into a circle or something easy that the horse enjoys.

sideways towards your goal but still *think* forwards as well as sideways. In the beginning, the horse may bring his shoulders rather too much to the inside as he is drawn back to the track. This is not nearly such a bad fault as leading with the quarters, so be extra careful with your indirect aids.

FEEL WHAT YOU SEE!

As with all these things, timing and feel rule every small action of the legs and hands. Baucher's mantra of 'hands without legs, and legs without hands' is now taken to a further degree as described by his disciple Faverot de Kerbrecht (see final Classical Quote at the end of this chapter).

I am constantly amazed that more riders do not use their *eyes* to read their horse. Looking through our horse's ears with soft eyes not only keeps us centred, but also aware. The smallest irregularity can be perceived and

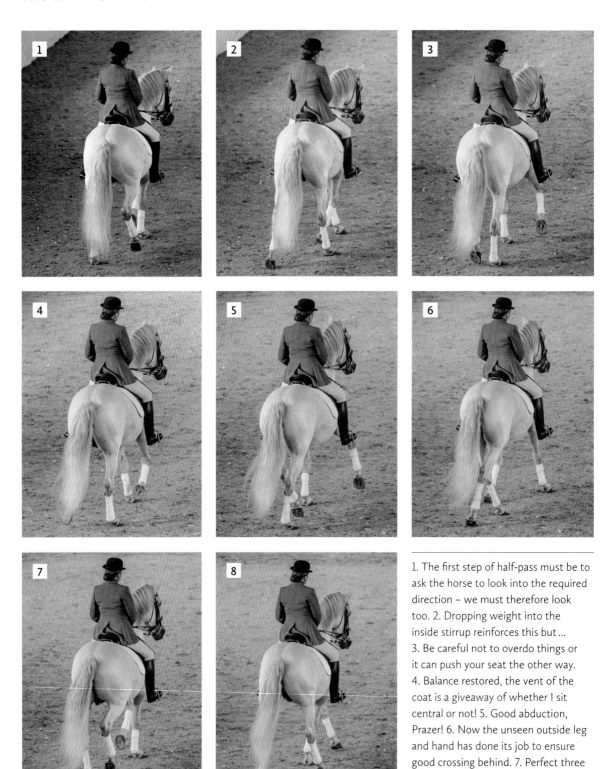

1. The first step of half-pass must be to ask the horse to look into the required direction – we must therefore look too. 2. Dropping weight into the inside stirrup reinforces this but... 3. Be careful not to overdo things or it can push your seat the other way. 4. Balance restored, the vent of the coat is a giveaway of whether I sit central or not! 5. Good abduction, Prazer! 6. Now the unseen outside leg and hand has done its job to ensure good crossing behind. 7. Perfect three tracks! 8. Nice crossing in front to finish on a good note – thank you Prazer!

immediately corrected until it becomes subconscious – particularly when it relates to bend and straightness.

It is a well-known phenomenon that horses feel when our gaze is upon them. I believe this leads to a telepathic understanding between horse and rider. Watching and connecting with your horse will finesse your aiding skills until they become subliminal.

THINGS TO GUARD AGAINST

In shoulder-in, don't turn your head to look down the track (even if you are told to!) since this will displace your weight and confuse your horse. (It may also rick your back...) Your head is quite heavy, about 12–13 pounds – and it must stay aligned to your horse. Your eyes after all can still look down the track.

In travers and half-pass, it is all too easy for the horse to confuse the aid of the outside leg with that of canter. Try to make the sideways feel slow and steady rather than quick, light and active – as in canter.

THINK POSITIVE

The feel of lateral movement will be much improved if you first walk each movement on the ground. Follow a line on your carpet or yard and place your body in the correct angle. Then, with hands on hips to keep your back supported, explore the sideways sensation. Back on the horse, think of how you would ride a straight line across the diagonal and how you naturally support him to the outside; then mimic this for your first steps of shoulder-in.

CLASSICAL QUOTES

'There exists a constant co-operation between the legs and the hands, which instead of opposing one another, should on the contrary, combine, harmonise and strengthen their effects.'

— BLAQUE BELAIR, FRENCH SCHOOL

✦

'By his hands and legs, helped by his eyes, the rider ought to be able to feel the actions and above all things, the tendencies of the jaw, head, neck and shoulders.'

— FILLIS, ENGLISH SCHOOL

✦

'Although the shoulder-in and the croup to the wall should be used jointly and are excellent for imparting suppleness, a handsome curve and good posture, the lesson of the trot on a straight line and on circles should not be abandoned.'

— LA GUÉRINIÈRE, SCHOOL OF VERSAILLES

✦

'The indirect rein which is used to produce the half-halts or vibrations must be used most delicately as the intensity of its action must never be greater than the horse's resistance.'

— DECARPENTRY, SCHOOL OF SAUMUR

✦

'The inside rein maintains position [in the shoulder-in] and the outside rein defines the degree of the position and leads the horse in the desired direction.'

— PODHAJSKY, SCHOOL OF VIENNA

'Each time that the hindquarters do not move actively enough sideways, it is the opening of the outside rein in the opposite direction of the half-pass which corrects that tendency.'

— OLIVEIRA, PORTUGUESE SCHOOL

✦

'It is by placing all the parts of the horse in the most exact order that the rider will easily communicate the impulsion which will produce the regular movement of the legs.'

— BAUCHER, FRENCH SCHOOL

✦

'Precise and delicate rein-effects are impossible without full and frank acceptance of the bridle by the horse. And there can be no full acceptance of the bridle without generous impulsion, adequate for the movement with something to spare.'

— WYNMALEN, DUTCH SCHOOL

✦

'There comes a time in the training and the management of the trained horse when the effects of the legs must be united to those of the hands. This comes about very naturally and without danger of lack of accord, because the training has then reached the point where aid-application is a mere nuance.'

— FAVEROT DE KERBRECHT, FRENCH SCHOOL

CHANGING THE BALANCE

Lengthening and Extension

ONCE WE HAVE BEGUN to bring the horse's weight back, we are then in a position to invite lengthening, which will take us on the path towards the medium and extended gaits. When I used to compete with young horses, I could never understand why the demand for lengthening came long before those collecting exercises which would draw the hind legs further underneath, thus setting them up for it.

Unrealistic expectations often lead to riders literally chasing their horses around the arena. Speed is *very* different from impulsion. Clearly, without the necessary engagement and strength behind, whatever the front end can produce will not be matched by the hind legs. Rushing the horse before he is ready invariably leads to him dropping onto the forehand or going wide behind so the forelimbs bear the brunt.

'THROUGHNESS'

Lengthening requires a greater degree of suspension than in the working gaits and this relies on strong, active hindquarters. This will lend a pleasant 'uphill' look to the gait. The extension of both fore and hind legs should be evenly matched. Too much foreleg action generally denotes a horse on the forehand and, without meaningful engagement behind, there will be little or no lengthening throughout the horse's frame. The 'throughness' of the movement should emanate from good hock action, pass over the horse's

An elastic contact allows Q to extend her frame as well as her stride. Sitting tall and quiet – no pushing – a quick press of my legs gives extra reach. In dressage jargon, 'perfect As' means the angles of the fore and hindlegs perfectly match, thus indicating good balance.

back and seek the contact via supple shoulders. The horse must neither lean on the bit nor drop behind it.

JUDGING GUIDANCE

It should be very easy to define a correct medium or extended trot. The whole horse – nose to tail – should appear longer and slightly higher – proof he is stretching forward to meet the rider's hand and carrying himself. This is our first priority. Lack of tension is another. A flowing, swinging tail denotes a 'happy' back. Ideally, the muzzle should be roughly level with the reach of the advanced forefoot. The lines of the diagonal legs should run parallel one to the other.

Topline muscling must extend over the whole frame if the horse is to carry the rider easily. Progressive stretch and flex exercises throughout the horse's training have hugely contributed.
1. Following the contact down with flexion helps support the horse's back.
2. Giving the contact away is very useful for total relaxation but be aware the horse is rather less supported under saddle.

TOP LINE

Few horses can extend fully without the necessary muscling over the back and quarters to allow the stretch while keeping it all together. A harsh, pushing seat is not conducive to the development of good muscle tone. Horses can only build up muscle through flex *and* stretch exercises and without sufficient stretches on the long rein in training, they are likely to be tight in the neck and back.

COILING THE SPRING

In Chapter 7 we discussed the concept of containing the horse's energy in collection. Once the horse has understood the meaning of the 'closed' or 'semi-closed' door, he will automatically understand the invitation of the open door. We coil the spring, by transferring weight behind. The more the hind limb joints flex and bend, the more we feel the energy starting to bubble up under and behind the saddle. For a split second, we retain this with a gentle half-halt – then, with a little rebalancing – we unleash and *fly*!

Horizontal thrust comes from the strong gluteals and hamstring muscles which push the hip joints further forward. Suspension and upward propulsion comes from well-developed stifle extensor muscles and well-flexed fetlocks and hocks. This is a lot for the horse to co-ordinate and sustain, so it is important only to expect a few lengthened strides at the onset – otherwise the balance will tip. Once mastered however, the horse will love it!

PREPARATION

By working quietly and patiently, step by step, the horse will gradually develop sufficient muscle power behind and under the saddle to hold himself in the required frame for longer. This requires good control from the rider's back too!

For me, the further schooling of the horse and his subsequent understanding is always about showing him the difference. The shoulder-in and other collecting exercises give him the strength and the means; it is now time to show him the way. *There must be light and shade in our approach, which is best introduced in the transitions.* It is by feeling the *contrast* that the horse learns – and we, in turn, can perfect the aids.

Shoulder-in on the corner is a very good exercise to set the horse up for lengthening across the diagonal from the next quarter marker. Your upper body angle should hardly have to change from that of the shoulder-in.

WHERE?

Traditionally, most dressage tests ask for medium trot on a straight line. The diagonal across the school is very inviting, because it offers a wide open space in which to open up the gait. Although this can be encouraging to a calm experienced horse, with a younger, more excitable animal, it can lead to explosive behaviour and a loss of balance. In this case, start by working alongside a rail or wall wherever possible. Using the corner to prepare is useful and a few sideways steps before you straighten up are very empowering. Later, on the diagonal, try riding almost to X collected and only lengthen in the second half. There must always be a balanced start and finish to the movement. Gradually, build up and increase the extended strides.

1. Try riding collected to a certain point on the diagonal line.
2. Now lengthen a few steps and then rebalance.
3. These transitions within the gait should be done with the seat aids, never the hands. It's all a matter of fine-tuning.

HOW?

Whilst little seems written on how to achieve good lengthening, the guidelines on how *not* to ask are clear in the classical books. There is the warning not to drive the horse out in front of you, which will only put him on the forehand. Too much leg is another no-no. The temptation is always just to go faster, but good extension is about better suspension. This requires we keep the horse on the bit but the contact must be carried forward as the neck lengthens.

Throughout, the fingers should continue to ask and give if the horse is not to 'fall apart'. With better engagement comes increased scapular movement, and alternate rein aids synchronised with those of the rider's legs can really encourage the horse. For example, as the horse's right shoulder moves forward, the right rein eases slightly to allow greater reach. By contrast the fingers of the left rein may squeeze or gently half-halt to support its opposite number.

UPPER BODY

A number of riders – even at the higher levels – adopt an extreme leaning back position to extend the trot, which appears to go hand-in-hand with shortening the neck. Bringing the upper body behind the vertical will only shift the rider's weight towards the rear. This may well open 'the door' – and with more weight on the two seat bones there is arguably more push – but if too much is pushed through, the horse will start to lose balance, thus tempting the rider

to draw back on the rein. (It is also possible that this drawing back and shortening the neck may be an entirely unintended consequence of the rider's upper body posture. Leaning back without making any accommodating adjustment of the reins will almost certainly lead to pulling.)

If the whole seat slips back as a result of slack abdominal muscles, the displaced weight of the rider may impinge on the correct interplay of the muscles over the equine loins. This would account for a high croup and tension in many horses. Often, the forelimbs are then

I would never normally ride like this except to show how *not* to ride since it drives the horse 'downhill'.

thrown out extravagantly – 'shooting the cuffs' – in an effort to 'catch' the balance. Unfortunately, there are still too many judges who favour these 'leg movers' even in higher-level dressage, and it should be recognised that this type of gait is biomechanically incorrect. For these horses, it will be very much harder to make good transitions into collection.

CORRECT DRIVING

Instead, I train my students to sit up and think of raising their centre of gravity before asking for bigger strides. Sitting tall helps to liberate the horse's forehand. With the horse lightly on the bit, I then ask for a tiny half-halt to prepare – and only then draw the shoulders slowly back to deepen the seat bones and push the waist towards the hands. In this way, an effective driving aid is applied from the *centre* of the saddle – not the back.

According to Decarpentry, the French maestro responsible for updating the FEI dressage rules, bringing the shoulders behind the vertical is only valid during the process itself. He states that staying there is counterproductive, an attitude with which I heartily concur.

On reaching the end of the diagonal or long side, we should have regained our vertical posture and the horse seamlessly regains his.

The setting-up of the horse for extended strides is the most important part of the process.
In 1. and 2. I raise my centre of gravity, ensure my seatbones remain in the centre of the saddle, close the leg and only then in 3, 4 and 5 allow more forward through my seat, back and fingers.

'LIGHTNING' TOUCH

Clearly, lengthening must be accompanied by the correct leg aids. As the shoulders move back, it is easier for the rider's legs to contact the girth area. In trot, some riders prefer to use diagonal aids initially. A touch with the spur from say, the left leg will stimulate the left hind leg as it is about to step under, but generally I prefer to ask for lengthening with both legs acting together.

We have already discussed, the dampening-down effect of the legs moving back behind the girth, so nagging here in the hope of achieving bigger strides, is counterproductive. Instead, we need to open the door! The placing of the leg aid is very simple. Just as we humans are tickly under the armpit, so is the horse. It is the use of the rider's inner leg just behind this spot – ironically called the horse's 'elbow' – which will elicit the right response.

A quick close and release of pressure at this point, really works! The late, great Nuno Oliveira spoke of 'electric shocks'. Simply think 'on-off' with both legs, then immediately allow them to drop back into a neutral hanging position the moment the horse responds. Remember the less you aid, the less you interrupt the flow.

In *Equine Biomechanics for Riders*, Karin Blignault points out that 'the intercostal nerve's most superficial area is in front of the girth'. She also suggests that it may be hard for some riders' legs to contact this area. Having long legs, I've personally not had a problem with this – a 'lightning' touch at this sensitive spot having helped me achieve good lengthening even with horses not naturally gifted in this way. Nevertheless, if all riders sat in the time-honoured

This frame shows Q's hindlegs actually doing more than the forelegs. A rare sight in dressage tests today! The near hind strikes the ground ahead of the off fore due to a higher forehand. This picture would be improved with a longer neck, but having inadvertently slipped back in the saddle, Q is making a lovely job of it (despite the jockey).

manner as close to the pommel as possible, their legs could still contact the area directly above the girth which is equally reactive, according to my students (and their horses!).

ADVANCED DIAGONAL PLACEMENT IN TROT

The more 'uphill' the horse, the more the likelihood of advanced diagonal placement (ADP) of the hind legs. This occurs when the hind hoof contacts the ground a couple of milliseconds before the diagonally opposite foreleg. This should *not* necessarily be considered a fault since the horse is merely pushing a fraction earlier in the stance phase, bringing lift and energy to the trot. In the world of veterinary science and biomechanics, this is known as 'positive diagonal placement' since greater elevation of the forehand and deeper engagement behind is obviously recognised as a good thing.

Unfortunately, not everyone knows the difference between (positive) ADP and its negative counterpart where the forefeet contact the ground before the hind. Clearly this is a disadvantage and one of the signs is forging. It generally happens with horses who are not yet sufficiently engaged.

As with most things, teaching the horse to lengthen and eventually extend is a step-by-step process. Working on a big circle – half collected, half lengthened – will help the engagement process and make a refreshing change from straight lines.

CANTER

In canter, it's important to make sure the horse is nicely forward, supple, off the leg and straight before you consider any form of medium canter or extension. Working canter must be well established, with the horse very responsive to your canter aids. Opening the canter up can only evolve from a degree of collection. It is all too common for the horse to rush if you ask too much, so just work towards four or five longer strides to start.

1. As in the trot, use the corner to rebalance.
2. A few steps of shoulder-fore prior to turning across the diagonal will set the horse up nicely for medium or extended canter.
3. Remember to keep more weight into the inside (right) stirrup to support the forehand and straighten the horse.

147

The half-halt is an important precursor. If you allow too much with the reins, the horse is likely to drop onto the forehand in response to the driving aids. Instead, as with trot, bring your shoulders back to 'open the door', think 'uphill' and simply ease the fingers and elbows.

When lengthening on the diagonal, prepare the horse on a corner or circle with a slight feeling of shoulder-fore before taking your line. Only ask for lengthening once the horse has straightened. Take care to build up the strides gradually and over time.

THINGS TO GUARD AGAINST

- Looking down is a very common fault when asking for medium or extended gaits.

- Pushing with the seat may well push the horse out of rhythm and onto the forehand. He already has to take more weight on the forelegs to lengthen, so don't add to that!

THINK POSITIVE

It's vitally important that you retain an 'uphill' quality to both the trot and canter gaits in lengthening. Point your core towards the horizon when you ride – and let the energy come up and over the back. The leg aids should be light and quick so they don't impede the gait and, in the case of canter, press rather firmer with the *inside* leg than normal to lift the withers.

CLASSICAL QUOTES

'When the contact is strong, the horse will be pulling with his forelimbs but when the contact is light, the horse will push with his hind limbs.'

— BLIGNAULT, SOUTH AFRICAN SCHOOL

✦

'Great care should be taken not to change the pace too early or too suddenly; i.e. not to attempt the middle trot. It must all be done step by step, and it is most important never to lose the quiet, regular, forward stride.'

— MÜSELER, GERMAN SCHOOL

✦

'The more successful we are in relieving the dorsal muscles of the work of actual load-carrying, so they can oscillate freely and elastically the longer, springier and better timed will be the gaits. To achieve this, the rider must refrain from interference with the activity of the back.'

— SEUNIG, GERMAN SCHOOL

✦

'When, due to his conformation, one can only expect a limited extension from a horse, one should, if the movement is correct and rhythmic, evaluate this performance as highly as the impressive lengthening of a horse that was born with this talent.'

— ALBRECHT, SCHOOL OF VIENNA

✦

'When lengthening, the hand passive, but supple within its fixety, must give the horse a firm, elastic and continuous feel, without ever destroying impulsion.'

— DECARPENTRY, SCHOOL OF SAUMUR

✦

'By turning on a diagonal, a horse may offer a longer, more floating stride. The rider should not merely permit such an initiative by harmonizing with it, but rather encourage the horse to maximize the delivery of his own ideas!'

— DE KUNFFY, HUNGARIAN SCHOOL

✦

'The action of the legs should be interrupted as soon as it has been obeyed.'

— PAILLARD, SCHOOL OF SAUMUR

✦

'Follow and amplify the lengthened strides with your seat and push very little with your legs, because they sometimes make the horse lose his rhythm.'

— KOTTAS, SCHOOL OF VIENNA

REFINING THE WEIGHT AIDS

Flying Changes

B Y NOW, WE SHOULD have perfected our understanding of the forward aids, the bending and lateral aids, how to collect and store energy and how to increase the stride. The basic canter aids have already been described, including those for counter-canter and half-pass.

Whilst it is possible to teach the horse to change legs before he is fully collected, it must be recognised that this is a hit-or-miss area. We see showjumpers powering on between jumps and automatically changing legs of their own volition on corners and turns, but this is often random and with no guarantee of synchronicity. To avoid bad habits such as changing late behind or allowing the horse to become disunited, it is better to wait until we have achieved good balance and a solid foundation in all the exercises described to date.

The beauty of this increased suppleness and strength behind lies in the fact that the horse can now respond to each request immediately and easily. When it comes to changes on demand, *timing is key*. As the conventional aids are backed up – or eventually replaced – with a subtle weight aid, there is no mistaking the right moment. As always, 'less is more' is the general rule, but even then some horses can get worried or wound up, no matter how careful the rider.

Sitting tall, upright and calm should invite greater confidence in collection.

REDUCING THE BASE OF SUPPORT

It is not always understood that the more collected the horse, *the more precarious his base of support*. This requires a lot of trust – the horse is literally putting himself at our disposal – so we must treat this with respect.

If you have difficulty with this concept – then consider the opposite. A young horse at halt with a rider on his back will generally try to spread his weight over all four limbs. You could compare the balance to that of a table – a leg in each corner. This is a very safe position from the horse's point of view. Clearly, the dynamics will change once movement is involved but, if the rider moves about too much, the horse will simply spread the balance as much as possible. This accounts for hind legs 'camped out', forehand heavy, long, strung-out frame, and so on.

At the other end of the scale is the fully collected horse. The more elevated the gait, the more the horse will need to draw his hind legs closer to

his centre of gravity. The frame will appear to shorten as the back is raised, the neck arched and the croup tucks under. In fact the extensor muscles are now stretched to their limit but provided we ourselves stay erect and central to the movement, the horse will feel safe. He begins to trust us, to give us the balance so necessary for the introduction of changes which must always start in the hind legs (see above).

Flying change from right to left from two different angles show: (ABOVE LEFT) the position of my new 'outside' leg and (ABOVE RIGHT) in almost the same moment the deepening position of the new inside leg.

SUPPLENESS

None of this will happen naturally unless the horse continues to remain as relaxed as possible in the poll and jaw, which includes the muscles of the tongue and lips. Putting too much pressure on the horse too early may cause stiffening in these two areas, which will have a knock-on effect on every joint, every muscle – from front to rear. Biomechanically, the horse will lose fluidity the more there is tension. The fact that many dressage horses, especially those bred for magnificent movement, continue to carry out all that is asked of them despite real discomfort in those vital areas is a testimony to the incredibly generous nature of horses.

CHANGES

It must now be obvious that requesting a change of lead in canter is one of the movements where extreme tact is a must. The moment of suspension is quite pronounced in canter so quiet, clear aids are of the essence and the less you move your weight about, the better.

A really good rider will make flying changes look effortless and, with so much televised work at Grand Prix level now available to all, it is not always appreciated just what is involved. Once we break it down however there are at least five aspects to consider:

First – Straightness: we must appreciate that flying changes require the horse to free up through the shoulders for each and every change as the hind legs dictate, so avoid too much neck bend.

Second – Timing: we must be able to identify the moment of suspension when all four feet are off the ground in order to indicate that something is about to change.

Third – Action: within that nano-second, we must clearly invert or reverse the aids of seat, leg and hand in order to achieve a change.

Fourth – Enablement: we must allow the whole thrust or dynamic of the horse underneath to come through, before acting again.

Fifth – Balance: we, ourselves, must match the balance of the horse throughout.

All this has to happen in the twinkling of an eye.

PREPARATION

Unless we demonstrate skill in the timing of each change, then make the aids clear but complementary to the laws of gravity, the horse may mistake the request, get anxious or confused. Whilst all horses can conduct a flying change in the field, most do it with outside flexion and none of them are carrying anything up to 200 pounds in weight!

There are many excellent books which talk the rider through the different ways that we can set the horse up for teaching him the changes. Reducing the number of steps through the transition of walk-to-canter and canter-to-walk is the traditional way – others include riding a figure of eight, asking on the diagonal, from counter-canter on a bend, from half-pass back to the track and so on.

OPPOSITE PAGE
Keeping ourselves and the horse straight and level is the biggest challenge as we prepare for the first change of leg. In photos 1., 2. and 3. my (right) inside leg can just be seen at the girth supporting the right lead and my weight clearly into the right stirrup. The moment of suspension occurs somewhere between photos 4. and 5. where my left leg moves forward and the unseen leg requests a change of lead (from the right hind). Photo 6. shows left canter and weight into the left stirrup – although a moment later everything will reverse for the next change of leg.

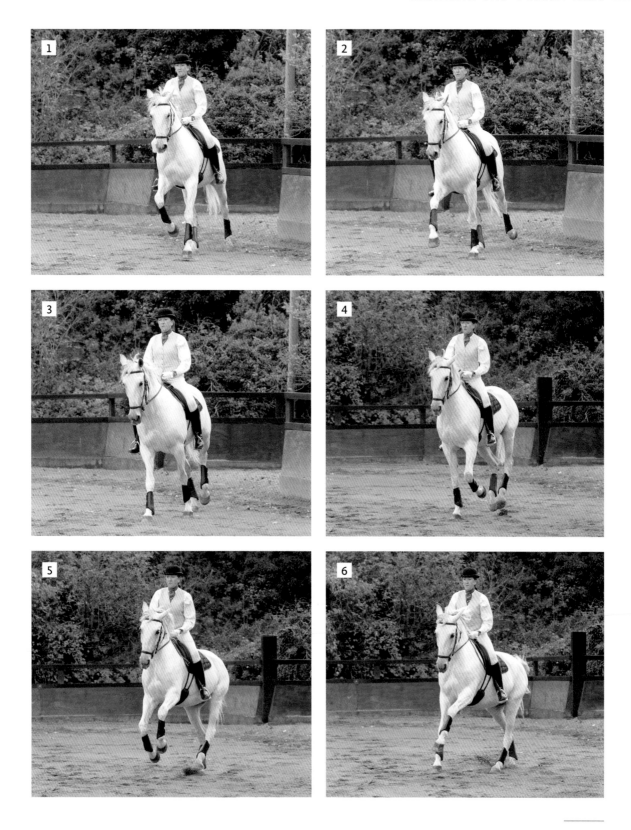

All are possible but the most important thing is not to expect too much too soon or to find fault if the horse fails to understand. I would strongly recommend *Kottas on Dressage* for a unique insight into the various options. My own *Dressage in Lightness* also goes into the subject in some depth from the horse's point of view and what he needs to feel from us. It must be recognised that every horse is different and conformational aspects can help or hinder the process.

SAME DIRECTION

Before we can assume that the horse will understand our aids for a change of leg, we must be absolutely sure he responds with certainty and confidence to each 'normal' canter request. He should be able to canter from walk and from rein-back on either rein. Whichever lead is requested, the rider basically needs

Riding forward and sideways is a very good exercise for cementing how much or how little we need to do to keep the horse responsive and to reinforce our canter aids. Finessing these will make your changes much easier. Here, I experiment with a few steps of canter half-pass and a few steps straight by alternating the sequence. Whatever we are doing – stay centered with the same leg position throughout. It is just a question of varying the pressures – downward or sideways.

to mirror the horse. *Our gaze, weight and energy need to be in the same direction as those of the horse in every phase of the canter.*

Before you start the changes, it helps to improve feel and awareness. Most of us are either right- or left-legged, a factor which comes to light when we experiment on the ground. Skipping for the human with one leg leading is very akin to canter for the horse. Try making a right circle with right lead (dismounted) and then do the same thing to the left. Doing this 'on each rein' a couple of times will help you identify how your weight transfers into the lead foot as it contacts the ground.

It is exactly the same when we apply weight into the inside stirrup to lead the horse into the canter and indeed to maintain it. Automatically, the outside leg should swing back. The legs should quietly retain that position whether going forwards or sideways until we want to change the gait.

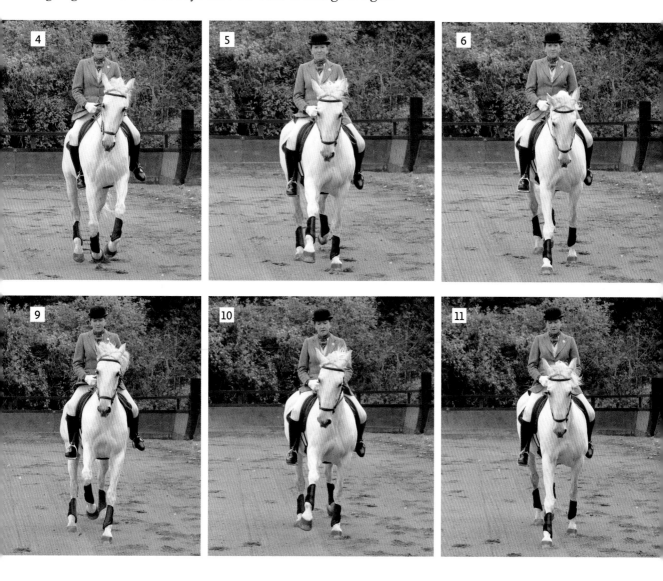

RIGHT OR LEFT?

Generally, right-legged people find canter left easier both off and on the horse. Once in the saddle, it will be their more active right leg that activates the horse's outside (right) hind, not only for the strike-off but for all subsequent driving power. It's also the leg responsible for guarding the quarters. As a consequence of our own one-sidedness, the more passive left leg should naturally 'hang' at the girth. This allows a little more pressure to drop into the left stirrup so the horse can follow our weight. It will also be the supporting leg in bends and turns.

Problems occur when a rider who is right-leg dominant changes the rein. On the right rein the dominant right leg may find it harder to let go, drop to the girth and lead. The left leg may be less proactive and 'forget' to move back to encourage the outside hind. This is often the cause of horses going disunited on a circle, trying to change when they haven't been asked to, or simply failing to offer the correct lead on request.

If we are ever to move on to flying changes, it is vital that these inconsistencies are recognised. The aids need not be big, but they must be clear. In order to improve our own one-sidedness, work on the ground can be invaluable. Once we ourselves learn to be ambidextrous, the horse has a chance to do the same.

BACK IN THE SADDLE

The key to successful changes has to be good departs on either rein, from any gait, at any time. Make sure in canter right for example, that:

- you have advanced your right (inside) hip

- weighted your inside seat bone

- placed pressure on your inside stirrup

- made sure your foot doesn't shoot in front of the vertical

- allowed your inside ankle to flex as you 'step down' into each new lead.

You might be surprised how many experienced riders do not necessarily do all these things – which is why it is so hard for them to make their changes easy for the horse. Clearly, to bring about a change in your horse's body, there has to be the correct change in yours!

INVERTING THE AIDS

Inverting the aids from, say, canter right to canter left should start in our seat. We must sit up, as quiet and centred as possible if we are not to confuse the horse. Clearly, the correct positioning of legs will not be effective without the correct positioning of our hips but these movements are subtle. Once we advance and weight the new inside (left) seat bone, the new outside hip and leg should automatically free up to stimulate the horse's (right) hind. In this way we replicate Nature – rider's hips to horse's hips – while still continuing to support the horse through our own good posture.

STEP INTO THE CHANGE

As you prepare for each change of leg, remember all you are doing is inviting the horse to move into your balance. Using the stirrups in this way allows gravity to pass down over the front of your thigh, through the knee and into the ball of the foot – hence the weight aid. For each change of leg, simply think of stepping a little forward and down – into the new leading leg, but beware of pushing against the stirrup – this will harden the thigh and take your weight in the opposite direction. Work with gravity, not against it.

LIGHTEN TO THE OUTSIDE

As the outside leg swings back, be aware that you have lightened the outside seat bone so the horse can come through from behind. With the younger horse, it may help to bring the shoulders slightly forward as you look over the new leading leg. This makes it easier to apply the outside aid behind the girth,

A flying change from right to left canter requires looking into the new direction and easing the process by lightening my right seatbone as the right hind pushes off. Once counter canter is established continue to look over the horse's leading leg and sit up.

so the horse can push off with confidence. At a later stage, you can begin to sit a little deeper into your changes, but in the early days, it really helps the horse to feel that he can make the change behind without impediment.

The dynamics of the change can make it hard to stay in balance, especially on a young, enthusiastic or big-moving horse, but if you concentrate on staying centred and using your stirrups and weight aids appropriately this makes things much easier for the horse and much easier for you!

REIN AIDS

Whatever the rein, the horse should always be slightly flexed from the poll in the direction of the leading leg. This means he will move with the inside shoulder and inside hip slightly in advance of their opposite number. The rider will reflect this natural posture, which is why it is so important not to over-turn the shoulders to the inside, but rather to look between the horse's ears.

Prior to each change, always sit up and apply a gentle check or half-halt on the outside rein. This not only straightens your horse but will alert him to the fact that something is about to happen. Then – as your leg aids invert and the horse pushes off from the required hind leg, the same rein must immediately soften forward again to allow sufficient stretch. You should also be looking gently into the new direction.

Provided your timing is good, the horse will begin to trust the rein aids, and by association may even be trained in time to make the changes in response to these alone – but only at a very advanced level of riding.

Here, in canter half-pass, three distinct tracks are shown as Prazer bends round my inside leg and moves away from the outside rein and leg.

MULTIPLE CHANGES

Obviously, multiple changes of lead should be introduced progressively. Using the serpentine is a good way to start, later in decreasing sequence on the diagonal line. The horse will need to remain straight and calm throughout. He should also be able to resist the opportunity to change when you set him challenges in counter-canter.

Throughout the changes, wherever and however you set them up, the seat, leg, weight and rein aids will remain exactly the same. They should at least have halved in intensity from the early days and by now, you may be using the outside leg less and less.

With a horse that is truly 'on the aids', a simple application of pressure into the new, leading stirrup may be sufficient for the flying change to take place. (See quote pages 164 and 180.)

ONE-TIME CHANGES

Clearly, with the tempis, there's little time to prepare, it's more a thinking process. A horse who is well tuned in to his rider may even respond to the deepening of the inside seat bone or weighting the stirrup alone. Others listen for the half-halt, still others to a mere nod of the head. It's important to remain focused, keep the horse together but not over-collected, and forward-thinking at all times.

Be very quick to reward and never ever chide when the horse is unable to give you what you want. Short-coupled horses, or those with a heavy neck and shorter shoulder will find changes harder than a more horizontally built horse such as those with Arab or Thoroughbred blood – today's Warmblood being a very obvious example. There are other higher-level movements which are just as enjoyable to teach and often it's a matter of taking a step back to work at what the horse is good at rather than aiming for the impossible.

THINGS TO GUARD AGAINST

It can be very unbalancing for the horse when the rider turns the shoulders as they look over the leading leg in each change. This will adversely affect the positioning of your inside hip and once you lose this, your leg aids lose efficacy. Before you know it the horse may disunite or simply refuse to change. Simply turn your face but keep your upper body as quiet and central as possible. Sitting down hard to push into the change is more likely to make the horse late behind. Instead, lighten the outside seat bone.

THINK POSITIVE

Looking over the horse's leading leg will always complement the canter, whichever rein you are on. Act like a horse; flex from the poll. Rotating your head from the atlas joint allows you to look into the required direction without disturbing your shoulder position, which must mirror the horse.

CLASSICAL QUOTES

'Flying changes should not be started until the horse is calm in the canter and can strike off from the walk on each hand with great ease.'

— OLIVEIRA, PORTUGUESE SCHOOL

'The proper time [for introducing changes] is when the horse has become free, supple, light and well balanced in all paces, obedient and above all things, attentive to the aids.'

— FILLIS, ENGLISH SCHOOL

'Beware, sometimes people who have ridden endlessly in counter canter then find it difficult to get the horse into change mode.'

— HESTER, ENGLISH SCHOOL

'The flying change of lead is a fresh canter depart inside the canter.'

— OLIVEIRA, PORTUGUESE SCHOOL

'When cantering with the off-fore leading, the horse's right shoulder and his right hip are somewhat in advance of his left shoulder and left hip. The feel of this position is transmitted to the rider's seat and the sensitive rider will adjust by intuition in conformity with the feel given him by his horse.'

— WYNMALEN, DUTCH SCHOOL

'The change itself – the inversion of the aids – has to be done with a minimum amount of physical movement or pressure. Your aids have to be precise, fast and light.'

— KOTTAS, SCHOOL OF VIENNA

'The controls for shifting and changing leg position must occur in this sequence (even though hardly distinguishable in point of time) at the instant the diagonal alights, for then the horse will change at the moment of suspension that follows the push-off of the inside front leg.'

— SEUNIG, GERMAN SCHOOL

✦

'Finally the canter can be indicated simply by a movement of the foot from the ankle with a fractional increase of weight on the stirrup, and the seat aid becomes superflous.'

— BURGER, GERMAN SCHOOL

✦

'The pressure of the foot in the stirrup is the minimum form of impulsive action of the leg on the perfectly schooled horse. The latter is achieved purely by lowering the toes, or opening the ankle joint.'

— DECARPENTRY, SCHOOL OF SAUMUR

11

THE HIGHER AIRS

The Aids of the Upper Body; Pirouette, Piaffe and Passage

As we have improved our technique, honing and refining the aids throughout our schooling – particularly with the more collected movements – we should have developed a heightened sense of our responsibilities. If our training has been correct, the horse will have entrusted his balance to us. Clearly, the way in which we sit and how we use the aids affects not only our own centre of gravity, but that of the horse.

In Chapter 10, we contrasted the horse with his weight spread out and a low centre of gravity with that of the collected horse. Now picture the High School rider – how upright the posture, how centred, how *quiet*. The concept of the centaur springs to mind. The rider sits tall, the horse grows tall. With his hocks tucked deeper underneath his frame, the withers rise, and consequently the head and neck. With a higher centre of gravity all round, the horse displays the same loftiness as his rider.

FRAGILITY

What may be less obvious is that the higher the centre of gravity, the more fragile the balance. This is why the horse will generally respond to the slightest aid, the *subtlest* change of weight. With the base of support rendered less stable, this can be used to the rider's advantage. In fact, it seems the rider can make their horse do anything with scarcely any effort – because it all so finely tuned.

A two way stretch – up from the abdominals to the breastbone and down through the front of the thighs to deepen the seat – promotes a stable, centered position. Squared low-set shoulders help open the upper body.

CORE STABILITY

In Chapter 7, we discussed how our abdominal muscles – extending up to the sternum and down to the pubic bone – affect the position of our seat in the saddle. By the same token, the very act of opening and squaring our shoulders will lengthen our front line and deepen the seat bones. This is akin to firming up, toning, 'finding the centre' and all the other popular phrases used in training today – but the main object now is to raise the centre of gravity.

Insufficient riding instructors focus on the aids of the upper body and how our back is affected by our front and vice versa. There is a fashion in dressage today to lean back, but losing verticality weakens our position – especially if the pelvis tilts back at the same time. Without firm core muscles, it is very easy to lose balance by so doing.

Equally misguided is collapsing the chest or the waist, or both. Slumping pulls the spine out of its natural 'S' shape, and over time, such a posture can do untold damage to the unprotected discs. Unfortunately, despite all the evidence to the contrary, there are still instructors around who tell their students to tuck their tails underneath them with the idea that they will go with the horse. 'Go' they certainly will … unbalanced and behind the movement too! All influence is lost except through the reins. The trouble begins when they want to stop, change things or collect – their position has made them ineffective.

THE RIDER'S BACK

In simple language, the human spine is not as straight as is often supposed. It is built with three distinct curves – two convex curves at the shoulders and hips and one concave curve or hollow at the waist. *These combine to give us spring, elasticity and protection in movement.* Flattening the back out of its natural 'S' shape is not at all the same as sitting up straight – quite the reverse. If we sit up straight correctly, the invisible gravity line which indicates our verticality will pass through our centre – as in standing tall.

If we are to progress to the higher airs, we must keep the waist forward and sit proud. Not only will this keep our weight central, but the natural contours of the spine will be supported. This gives us that 'allowing' feeling which protects our back from all the movement the horse sends up at us. It also stabilises us against centrifugal force and the forces of acceleration. Yet, too often we hear a riding teacher berating a pupil for being 'hollow' in the back when they are simply erect.

If we are unable to flex through the back, we have little hope of riding 'waist to hands' as promoted by the great Masters. It is this which allows a quiet but forward thinking hand.

Nevertheless, there is good hollowness and bad hollowness. Provided the rider's pelvis is upright, as in walking – there is nothing wrong and everything right about preserving the natural 'S' shape. In the higher airs, we may wish to accentuate the 'S', but never at the expense of impulsion. Too much lordosis (hollowness) may tilt the pelvis out of the vertical, thus putting on 'the handbrake' – although sometimes we may need this!

FULL SEAT

The seat of a good dressage rider will become increasingly sensitive to all these nuances as, together with their horse, they progress up the Scales of Training. The full seat is one which is elegant, deep and firm and which can resist any tendency of the horse to lean. Sitting heavy is not at all the same as sitting full-seated and is generally inappropriate, except in a pulling horse. By sitting tall and as close to the horse's strongest point as possible we have the power to

The 'Xenophon seat' promotes the image of the standing figure and happens quite naturally here as we stand to address an audience.

stop, start and make changes as and when required. There should come a point when the reins seem almost superfluous.

In each and every movement, minute shifts of weight will invite greater spontaneity from the horse. We have already discussed the importance of weighting the right or left seat bone to indicate direction and bend, and the driving aids of the seat bones for extension. By the same token, we now discover that deepening the front of the pelvis and dropping more weight into the thighs can bring about a collecting or gathering effect. It will also lighten the load on the back of the saddle.

The horse will naturally follow our weight back if we gently tip the pelvis just as we would for walking backward ourselves. Quietly close the leg behind the girth for each backward step and never pull the head in.

TEACHING THE HORSE TO 'SIT'

Progressing now to the higher level work, the rein-back is invaluable as a preparation for piaffe, passage and ultimately, the airs above the ground. Piaffe is a diagonal movement, so is rein-back. Oliveira used this exercise a great deal to engage the horse behind and writes: 'To rein back with the horse that has not lowered his hindquarters sufficiently, it can be very beneficial.' In other words, it allows us to close the angles behind the saddle in order to provide more spring and lift.

Of course, we should never progress to any of this work until the horse is extremely well engaged and light in the hand in all forward work. You may already have taught your horse to bring the hocks deeper underneath in halt. If not, gradually introduce this over a period of time with a very sensitive use of seat and leg.

In every movement, the rider's seat must be very discerning of its effects on the horse's back. Lightening the back of the seat frees up our legs to guide the horse in both his backward and forward progression. It also allows us to gather him a little more. With the loins released of pressure, the horse is less inhibited about dropping the croup and stepping deeper underneath. The more flexed the hind limb joints, the more lift to the forehand. Be very quick to release the rein at the first signs of tension.

PIAFFE AND PASSAGE

Somewhere, tied up within our feel for these aids – forward and back – lies the key to passage, piaffe and beyond. In his school near Mafra in Portugal, I remember seeing Oliveira on a comparatively young stallion riding two steps back, two very collected steps forward, three steps back, three even shorter steps forward. By the time he had requested this a third or fourth time, the horse was starting naturally to bend his joints, lift the forehand and offer the first few hesitant steps of piaffe. I use the same method today, always thinking forward out of the rein-back and into the piaffe and have found it very effective. It should go without saying that this must always be requested on soft reins with a forward-thinking hand.

Energy is everything at this point. Light 'asks' on the rein, coupled with quick, light 'asks' from the legs, helps us to activate but contain the impulsion being produced by well-engaged hind legs. As well as allowing the piaffe to progress forward, think now of drawing that vital source upward too. With subtlety, the walk steps will grow shorter and higher of their own accord. If we are lucky – and very patient – piaffe can eventually be ridden on the spot but this requires a very supple horse and a very balanced rider. The secret is to keep our own energy up! As we raise our own centre of gravity, the horse is given the freedom to elevate himself. In this way, more cadence and lift to the steps will naturally evolve.

Once the weight has moved back, we ask for piaffe. This shows promise since the raised foreleg is higher than the raised hindleg, the supporting foreleg is virtually straight, the croup is under and the forehand up. To be perfect, the nose should be a little more forward, but the poll (under the muscling) is the highest point.

At the first sign of tension – some horses may fizz up – release the rein forward which is often enough to restore harmony while retaining the movement.

All collecting requests must be subtle and short-lived. The seat aids simply echo the 'take and give' of the rider's hands and legs as described by the great Masters of Equitation (see Ch. 7). Be careful never to drive with your seat. Instead, *receive*. The moment the horse understands and begins to offer a couple of elevated steps, sit up, neutralise your position, and allow him to go forward again. This is very important. By constantly rewarding him in this manner, he will get stronger behind and want to offer more.

STEP BY STEP

Trot to halt, halt to trot transitions and more collection in between will help invite passage. Rein-back to trot is useful too. Take time. Again, we need a lot of energy for passage, but as with piaffe it has to be absorbed and contained within the balance of the movement. In asking for shorter, lighter trot steps, keep a very soft feel on the reins. Gentle half-halts applied alternately help transfer more weight to the quarters and, with greater bending in all the joints, the steps become higher. Every time you feel this, be very quick to make a *descente de main* (see Chapter 12) and praise.

In passage, it is often easier to start on a big circle, but never over-flex. Once the trot is collected and active, allow your legs to stretch back and down from open hips as though to scoop up the hind legs underneath. Again, light, active touches of the leg may be applied – alternately or together (depending on the horse) – a little behind the girth. With the former, the touch is generally applied just before each new engaging hind leg contacts the ground.

OPPOSITE PAGE AND BELOW This series, not necessarily in sequence, shows the start and end of passage on a curve with a few straight steps in between. The horse must remain on the bit throughout or flexion – so necessary for every single joint – would be lost. This does not mean that the degree of contact cannot change. Here, Prazer lightens himself on the rein, commensurate with the degree of flexion behind and subsequent liberation of the forehand.

The hands may also act alternately to collect and invite a more upward stride. For example, as the right fore is lifted, some riders may momentarily raise and squeeze the rein of the same side, while others half-halt to the opposite side. More important is the ability to release just as soon as the leg reaches forward and as always, timing will be of the essence. With some horses, it may help to take your shoulders very slightly forward of the vertical to lighten the seat; with others, the opposite. Think of your seat and core sucking the energy into an upward direction so you keep the energy bubbling away. With patience and tact, these movements will gradually evolve by themselves. Allow natural cadence to develop. Never force.

CANTER PIROUETTE

Once the horse has been progressively schooled to smaller circles and is able to execute these with ease – the result of well-engaged hocks – we can prepare for canter pirouette. This is merely a progression of the work to date. Without good bend throughout his body, particularly in the canter half-pass – the horse simply cannot stay upright in the pirouette – it is a physical impossibility. Any reliance on the inside rein would indicate he is not yet ready to perform this physically taxing movement.

Assuming that the horse is light in front, deep behind and is able to make balanced transitions from canter to walk, the pirouette is now within reach. Basically, the aids for this movement are very similar to those for the quarter or half turn (in walk) on the hocks, or for riding a square. It will be the indirect influence of the outside rein that largely dictates the pirouette. It will also depend upon a perfectly placed inside leg (pillar of support) and correct weight aids applied through the seat and stirrups.

There can be no pirouette without an abundance of energy. As with piaffe and passage, we must simply harness and contain this to shift the balance back. A good way to start the movement is from canter half-pass, where already the horse will be engaged, bent around the rider's inside leg and responding to the sideways (indirect) effect of the outside rein and outside leg. Simply ride a canter half-pass on the diagonal to the centre line, half-halt and, instead of continuing forward up the school, start turning away to the opposite side.

Once the horse is light in hand on smaller circles, try reducing these with a feeling of quarters-in but be careful never to turn ahead of your horse, or draw back on the inside rein. Imagine an extra rib on the inside of your body and draw the horse ever inward by pressing down on your inside stirrup.

Despite an asking inside rein, the head must be free to rise to complement a higher neck carriage whilst the unseen outside rein guides the forehand around my inside leg. As the horse gets stronger, there should be more flexion in both hocks while the poll remains the highest point.

As the horse gets used to this, the weight aid of the rider's inside seat bone should be more pronounced – the outside rein more proactive. Gradually, as the horse grows stronger behind, the turn away becomes more angled until one day you may be able to return on the same diagonal (180 degrees).

FIRMING UP

Another way to progress the canter pirouette is from travers conducted within a big circle. Gradually you take it to an ever more collected stage, thinking forwards and sideways as you diminish its size. The idea is for the hind legs to describe a smaller circle than that of the forelegs so the horse continues with the hindquarters and forehand on two different tracks. Keep your inside hip forward as normal and maintain the three-beat rhythm as the hind legs push progressively under. Sitting up and resisting any temptation to lean, grow taller and firmer to the inside. Thinking 'up' really helps the horse lift at the withers and take more weight behind. He must be gently flexed into the inside rein, and you should continue to look through the ears.

The outside (indirect) rein will give gentle half-halts as it takes the shoulders forwards, sideways and round. The outside leg will energise the sideways progression of the hind legs but, without firm support to the inside, balance will be lost. Applying a quick press with the inside leg at the girth can do wonders for impulsion and lift. Any temptation to shorten the inside rein should be

Canter pirouette is a wonderful movement to ride. Focus on your horse's poll, never lose the canter rhythm, but think of it in slow motion. Sit proud and breathe!

resisted. As soon as a few steps are obtained, you should ride the horse forward and out of the circle. Introduce a feeling of fun by riding away into a big, open canter – a nice reward for the horse!

As with all the higher movements, progress modestly. First a couple of steps, then the quarter, the demi and eventually a full canter pirouette – but not for every horse. It will take time and patience and a lot depends on the horse's ability to sit. A vision of dancing on a 'dinner plate' springs to mind, but I would be equally happy with a large hula-hoop!

AIRINESS

As you advance in your own understanding, the horse will show you what works for him. Passage is only a very exuberant trot which grows in height and loftiness. Once the collected trot becomes more airborne, it transforms into a movement of controlled extension. It is very important that we do not sit heavily and inhibit these transitions. If ever *feel* was important, it is now.

To request passage from piaffe is relatively easy, because the horse is being released from a very small base of support into an upwardly mobile, forward gait. There is the added bonus of elastic recoil from a movement of extreme collection to help lift the horse and thrust him forward. Think of opening a bottle of champagne! For this reason it is often better to teach the piaffe first, remembering of course that the cork is still in place!

Pirouette (in part) is something horses do naturally at play in the field. The horse must be able to lift his head and neck for balance but, as with normal

The levade is a gift from the horse to a rider he trusts. In classical training, it is a natural progression from the piaffe. A straight horse, matching pairs of legs, an expression of integrity, what else can a rider ask for?

canter, there are upward phases and downward phases and we must be able to hold the rhythm of the canter if it is not to turn into a spin.

FINAL THOUGHTS

Provided your horse is well engaged and nicely muscled through the back and quarters, he should be able to lift with you, to follow the dance – whatever the movement – and merge his balance with yours.

We have now reached a point in riding when we should never ever have to push the horse to do anything for us. Instead, our aids merely *invite*, with an increased lift in our own bodies to complement the lightness in his.

THINGS TO GUARD AGAINST

- In rein-back and piaffe, the horse must be flexed very gently to the inside to keep the quarters straight. Any crookedness will force an unequal load onto the hind legs, which makes it virtually impossible for the horse to drop his croup and step under correctly.

- In passage, beware of squeezing with the legs. Any feeling of force from seat or legs to lift the horse's back will inhibit upward and forward movement.

- Turning ahead of the horse in the canter pirouette will abort it before it begins. We must remain vigorously 'lined up'; hips to hips, shoulders to shoulders. Beware of too much outside leg, which can turn the pirouette into a spin!

THINK POSITIVE

- In the higher airs, always reward the horse when he gives you what you want by releasing the contact with a *descente de main*. The more he can carry himself, the more brilliant the work.

- The *descente de jambes* – allowing the legs to drop – is an important training aid. It is most relevant when moving out of the rein-back, piaffe, passage or pirouette and returning to a forward 'normal' gait again. These rewards build the horse's self-esteem and increase his desire to offer more.

(*Descente de main* and *descente de jambes* are discussed in more detail in the next chapter.)

CLASSICAL QUOTES

'Before indicating backward stepping, the rider has to ensure collection at the halt. The necessity for correct leg aids at the halt prior to the rein-back is not appreciated by all riders but is nonetheless very important.'

— ALBRECHT, SCHOOL OF VIENNA

✦

'The rider displaces the centre of gravity of the mass – horse and rider – by altering his own position.'

— DECARPENTRY, SCHOOL OF SAUMUR

✦

'Balanced between the alternating forward urging aids and the restraining one, the horse finally learns to adjust his own centre of gravity to the centre of gravity of the rider; horse and rider are then transformed into a completely united system ... poised on a progressively decreasing area of support.'

— BURGER, GERMAN SCHOOL

✦

'Alternating forward and backward movement is a more useful form of gymnastics than the rein-back of itself. It develops especially the suppleness of the back.'

— DECARPENTRY, SCHOOL OF SAUMUR

✦

'Flying changes can be performed with less collection and less suppleness, whereas pirouettes, passage and piaffe will never succeed without a maximum of these qualities.'

— PODHAJSKY, SCHOOL OF VIENNA

'The piaffe in which the horse is tense, contracted and on edge is not the domain of equestrian art. It is a circus piaffe.'

— OLIVEIRA, PORTUGUESE SCHOOL

✦

'It is inadvisable to demand at the beginning anything more than the "soft" passage, which has a relatively small elevation; the resilience of the hocks has to be patiently developed.'

— ALBRECHT, SCHOOL OF VIENNA

✦

'A very high passage is brilliant, but it is not the height of the action which indicates the quality of the passage. It is rather the slowness, tied to the time of suspension.'

— OLIVEIRA, PORTUGUESE SCHOOL

✦

'If the hind feet step together [in canter pirouette] there is not enough impulsion.'

— KOTTAS, SCHOOL OF VIENNA

✦

'The stirrup aid is the last finishing touch, the ultimate refinement of the leg aid; a mere hint of an aid which becomes sufficient when total unity and equilibrium of horse and rider have been achieved.'

— BURGER, GERMAN SCHOOL

ONE-HANDED RIDING AND FINESSING THE REINS

THE TRANSFORMATION that has taken place in our horse as a result of the balance that our upper body and seat have rendered is a thing of wonder. Suddenly, there is an immediacy and ease in every transition, every request – hitherto never dreamed of. All at once, it is as though we hardly need the reins.

Of course such a statement is wishful thinking. Without that vital connection to the horse's mouth, we cannot indicate where we want him in space or indeed in what balance. The rein tells the horse not only where to look but how to use his hindquarters. It is the invisible link to the horse's power. The hand that knows how to collect and store the horse's energy under or behind saddle without seeming to do anything is a wise hand. So indeed is the hand that knows how to release the energy gradually or in delicate, intermittent 'gives' depending on how much we wish to keep in reserve.

But do we always need two hands? The proof of good riding surely has to be that the rider's body is responsible for the main aiding while the reins simply harness the energy which we now find at our disposal.

THE *MISE EN MAIN*

To go a little further – it is the channelling effect of *all the aids* that brings about what the French call the '*mise en main*'. This can only come about *when* the horse works to a superior level of gymnasticity *as though oblivious of the bit(s) in his mouth*. In truth, of course, the opposite is true! The horse *is* aware of the bit in his mouth, but he accepts it gladly. His mouth is moist and malleable in

Dropping the legs after moving out of passage – *descente de jambes* – invites the horse to normalise the gait. This may also be accompanied by a partial *descente de main* and you will feel when this is appropriate. Never 'drop' the horse unless he himself is in a good balance.

response to quiet, feeling hands. Once the poll and jaw are relaxed, the horse can carry himself in a good posture. It should be obvious that without supple joints and an equally good posture in our own bodies, the hands can never be steady enough to make the very fine adjustments required of them.

There is nothing more detrimental to the connection between horse and rider than hands that move in a backward direction – towards the rider's lap. Generally, this is caused by a stiff back which rebounds on every other joint. To develop lightness, we must be able to ride from the body to the hands, which requires us to flex through the lower back. This allows our centre and our energy to be drawn forward as though by an invisible string.

A SINGLE UNIT

Forward-thinking hands must never be confused with overtly 'following' hands as employed with the very young horse. On the fully trained horse, our body is carried forward by him as one unit and the hands are part of that unit. Any extra movement – other than the give and take of the fingers, the easing of the elbows, the flexion of the rider's back (all of which should be invisible) may well be counterproductive.

By now we should be able to make every bend, every turn, every figure and transition from the body alone. The hands held quietly opposite each other simply provide a funnel for the horse's energy. By this time, the distance between the rider's two fists will be no more, and preferably a little less, than the width of the bit. The image of the two hands in a velvet glove is helpful.

THE 'INSINUATING' HAND

Whether riding one- or two-handed, the action of the rein is dictated by our sense of *feel* for the balance of the horse at all times. Finger control, especially with the double reins, should be subliminal. The use of the little finger (some prefer the ring finger) on the bridoon becomes automatic; the use of the curb finger, more intentional, as and when required. The thumb lying fairly flat to secure the rein happens naturally. If we need to resist, we simply square the shoulders, set the elbows and wrists and push the stomach to the hands.

Since all delicate work with the fingers requires a point of reference, control may be enhanced when the base of the hands just touches the base of the

Riding one-handed should alter nothing. Here Prazer flexes left and remains on the bit from the different application of the fingers which will become automatic with practice.

horse's neck. (Think of work on a keyboard, or a fine piece of sewing … in both cases the hands rest). Lightly contacting the mane with the base of the little finger is the preserve of many a fine horseman or horsewoman, especially with regard to a delicate mouth.

DESCENTE DE MAIN

By this stage of schooling, the *descente de main* (first mentioned in Chapter 3) should have developed into a regular practice. This is rarely seen today in a high level dressage test and yet that is the very time when it is most appropriate. As Barry Marshall, experienced FEI judge and a former British *chef d'équipe* at the Barcelona Olympics writes: 'Sometimes, during a test you will see an experienced rider give and re-take with the inside rein. Although not part of the test, this should not be marked down. This giving and re-taking is of invaluable help to the rider as a test of the horse's self-carriage and, as such, may be a guide to you [the judge] also.'

In fact Decarpentry goes a step further and describes how once the horse is familiar with this action, it helps him to 'use all the resources of his instinct

The giving of the hand – *descente de main* – should only be made when the horse is in a good balance as shown here. '... The proper time to perform this movement is after a half-halt when you feel the horse coming back on its haunches.' La Guérinière, 1733.

to make good any local weaknesses of his muscular system and free his movements of any trace of stiffness.' Truer words were never said. Giving forward with the rein in this way should also encourage the horse to step deeper underneath himself. It also confirms to us, the rider, that he has no need of its support. It's a reward, a release but also a lovely proof that our horse carries himself.

TWO INTO ONE

If all these criteria are met, the transition from riding with two hands to one hand should be pretty effortless. As La Guérinière wrote in 1733, 'the height of the hand generally determines the height of the horse's head' and at a more advanced stage of training, the hand is consequently held higher in the more collected airs.

The traditional way of riding with one hand is to transfer both reins to the left hand so as to keep the right hand free to carry the stick (sword in the cavalry), which may be placed in different positions. In normal circumstances, the whip will lie at an angle across

ABOVE AND LEFT Carrying the whip across the breast is a very safe and practical way of mimicking the bearing of the sword. In the cavalry, this was described as 'protect and prepare' – ready for action!

the rider's thigh. For a salute or ceremonial, it may be held upright or at an angle across the rider's breast. In traditional Iberian fashion it is often held in this latter way.

DELICATE WORK

The position of the left (rein) hand is important. For normal forward, straight work it should remain central at all times – higher or lower according to the horse. Turning left will be easier than turning right since the position of the inside snaffle rein will lie under the little finger, which is very effective in inviting the horse in that direction. Turning right will require more tact, and a thorough understanding of the other aids at our disposal.

We must therefore be very clear with our opening aids and our indirect ones. By moving the hand very slightly to right or left, the inside rein(s) opens as appropriate, and in the same instant this brings the outside rein(s) to bear against the horse's neck (as in a neck-rein) in exactly the same way as would happen in two-handed riding. These very slight adjustments should automatically guide the forehand right or left.

With a finely tuned horse, finger control alone can bring about the same effects. In the double bridle, turning or asking for bend to the left will be requested by the little finger on the bridoon (i.e. the left side of the left hand). Right turn or right bend will be asked for by the forefinger.

This sequence shows a 180 degree turn around the hocks – or demi-pirouette. Riding one-handed highlights the beauty of the indirect aids as well as those of our weight. Again we must stay square to the horse in all the work. This exercise would be a good test of rider skills for instructor examinations.

Turning right with correct flexion requires rather more attention to finger control than on the left rein. Again, the aids of seat and leg must complement every request.

This leaves the action of the two curb reins to be controlled by the 'inner fingers' – the left curb by the ring finger, the right curb by the long 'middle' finger next to it. As in two-handed riding, the thumb lies flat over all the reins to secure the contact which should be no less, no more, than formerly. With the snaffle bridle, everything is rather simpler; and not everyone uses the little finger. The ring finger will serve equally – although it is arguably less sensitive.

ALL-ENCOMPASSING

An experienced rider who has never ridden one-handed before should find all this pretty automatic. Every rein aid works in conjunction with the normal weight aids of seat and leg and is more of a suggestion than a command. Yet the horse feels its influence keenly and the feeling through his mouth is our constant guide.

There should be no need to alter the length of rein except for the stretch. For normal work, we can collect a little more by raising the hand and bracing the back. For the medium and extended gaits, we generally lower the hand and consequently allow more through both the back and the elbows. For work on a long rein, we simply take the hand forward.

Even on a slacker rein, raising the hand gives lift to the forehand. In this passage, we can see the level of extension that takes place in this very elevated movement – the opposite of piaffe where we close the horse.

If your riding has been correct to date, you may be surprised how easily your horse adapts to one-handed riding. By this time he should be much more attuned to your weight aids. The hands, by this stage, have become the finishing touches for all the work to date. Although the action of each aid may achieve a different effect, e.g. opening inside rein, outside rein used indirectly (snaffle), direct flexion (curb) etc, it is the 'combined effect' – *l'effet d'ensemble* – beloved of the old Masters that transforms riding into an art.

All the individual aids must complement each other – e.g. the outside rein only mirrors what the outside leg does – acting against the horse to send him in the opposite direction. The inside aids, e.g. weight into inside seat bone or inside stirrup, mirror the inviting effect of the inside rein.

In my view, every dressage rider above Novice level should be able to ride a test one-handed. It is almost impossible to do this unless we ride from the centre; to my mind, an excellent way of improving rider skills.

For a moment, Prazer makes a jump out of levade – his very first attempt at courbette perhaps – but that is some way off. No one could have been more surprised than me – but the discipline must be the same – sit still, tall and look forward!

Even if you never ride a dressage test, riding one-handed is a good proof that your communication with the horse has been correct to date. It is a test of your own abilities and if there have been mistakes made along the way, riding one-handed will help to identify and correct them. It is also very pleasurable to do since it is a refiner of all the work covered to date, and horses often go better as a result of the rider's improved balance.

As the late, great Colonel Podhajsky wrote of the 1936 Olympic Games: 'The dressage test did justice to the principles of classical riding in every respect.... The rider was to guide his horse with the reins in one hand during some of the exercises. It was clear that this test was designed by men who themselves were capable of practically demonstrating on horseback what they expected from other riders.'

Doesn't that say it all?

And after all the work – complete release.

CLASSICAL QUOTES

'Temporarily riding with one hand offers great advantages not only with remounts, but also with horses that are already well ridden and with riders in all stages of training.'

— SEUNIG, GERMAN SCHOOL.

✦

'When riding with one hand the indirect rein acts alone – the direct rein becoming slack at the moment of action. If the two reins are not in absolute agreement, they at any rate, do not oppose each other.'

— BLAQUE BELLAIR, SCHOOL OF SAUMUR

✦

'When the horse is confirmed in the ramener[1] *he must be educated to the indirect lateral flexion ... which should be practised in motion and preferably at the trot. The rider requests lightness on one rein and having obtained this then carries his hand somewhat towards the opposite side, so that the rein bears against the base of the neck.'*

— DECARPENTRY, SCHOOL OF SAUMUR

✦

'Turning left ... the position of the inside rein, which is just below the little finger, affords ease in turning the horse towards the left, to which is added a natural disposition on the part of the horse to turn in that direction.'

— LA GUÉRINIÈRE, SCHOOL OF VERSAILLES

---

1 The *ramener* is the term used in the academic French School to refer to the collection of the horse's forehand and, according to Baucher, is the result of perfect flexions. This is in contrast to the *rassembler*, which generally applies to the collection of the hindquarters but is often used to indicate the collection of the whole horse.

'Alternating using the direct and the indirect effects of the same rein, the rider steers the horse on serpentines of gradually tighter loops and on figures of eight of gradually decreasing size. This work must be practised with each of the reins held separately.'

— DECARPENTRY, SCHOOL OF SAUMUR

'There are few persons who understand well how to use the right rein ... to turn the horse right, therefore, the control of the outside rein must be felt in the bridle-hand, so that the turn comes from the withers.'

— LA GUÉRINIÈRE, SCHOOL OF VERSAILLES

'Separation of the aids means that they should be implemented separately, as much as possible. This principle extends to the use of the reins, which should not contradict each other.'

— RACINET, FRENCH SCHOOL

13

PERFECT BALANCE
IN ALL THINGS

....

I F WE HAVE SCHOOLED our horse conscientiously over a respectable period of time – at least two to three years to roughly Elementary level and double that for the higher levels – we should have reached that point where everything we ask and everything we do is clearly and immediately understood by the horse. Each stage of the journey should have progressed both horse and rider to the next stage.

The positioning and the use of our aids and how the horse feels them on his body should gradually have become less conspicuous and more subconscious. With good timing, based on the principle of reward and release for every response correctly interpreted, the area over which the aids are applied will have narrowed down. For example, there will be less difference between the position of the rider's leg on the girth, leg in front of the girth or leg just behind the girth, yet the horse will respond to each nuance with alacrity.

The seat aids will be similarly discreet, and those of the hands even more so. The horse will be well acquainted with the indirect rein aids as well as the direct aids, he will naturally feel more comfortable flexed from the poll and all the work should have a seamless quality about it. Indeed, an onlooker will have to be extremely observant to see what the rider does to achieve a result.

Not every horse can be trained to advanced levels of dressage and this must be recognised. Breed type and conformation all play a part, as do history and temperament. There will be some horses who, for various reasons, may never have mastered clean changes, others for whom piaffe or passage is too much, still others who do not have the strength in the quarters for canter pirouette.

More important than the length of stride is the level of engagement behind. Flexibility and gymnasticity prolongs a horse's life if correctly prepared and practised with respect. There can be no ease of movement without a degree of poll flexion since every joint influences its neighbour and there will be no chain reaction throughout the body if a single part of the whole is out of synch.

Nevertheless, all should be able to offer both working and collected gaits, to include some lateral movements.

The quality and magnitude of the gaits is something else. Some horses with upright shoulders and naturally high knee action may never lengthen as impressively as we might wish, while others of the daisy-cutting variety may find collection much harder to sustain, except for short periods of time. The most important thing is that the gaits are well defined, even and light and that the horse has learned never to lean on our hand as he becomes more responsive to the influence of seat and leg. Improving his sensitivity to the aids by degrees has been solely our responsibility.

As training becomes more advanced therefore, it should be clear to any bystander that we have helped the horse to cope with our weight for whatever task is reasonably required of him. By the same token, it should be equally obvious that we have never hindered or overburdened him. It is important that the rider remains fit and flexible in their own body if the horse is to do the same. The correct balancing of the horse requires much self-discipline and insight, but our reward is a partner who conforms to each request with a willingness that is humbling.

Looking through your horse's ears must never be under-estimated. It gives us the cue and the clue for every move we make, every step we take. Horses know the moment we are not 'with' them. They make their own music and we should ebb and flow with them.

During our work, our understanding should have broadened. The old saying 'practice makes perfect' is very true, but horses dislike being drilled. Instead, we need to be versatile in our approach, interspersing the work in the school with hacking over undulating country and some modest natural jumps where possible. Reward and praise – positive reinforcement – plays a huge part in motivating the horse and should never be underestimated. I thank and praise my horse every day and it costs *nothing*.

For the serious work, the order of the day should depend very much on how the horse is feeling. We must never forget the basics so, some days, desist

Never forget the basics. Simple movements tell a thousand stories.

from riding 'movements' – or do them in different places – out in the field, for example! The walk should never be neglected as it is 'the mother of the gaits'. It is also the gait in which we supple every joint without duress and, if ridden in a good balance, it strengthens the horse behind. Horses should get used to standing quietly on long reins. In the old days some Master Horsemen would use that time to puff on a cigar ... how civilised!

There is no doubt that theory without practice or practice without theory is of little use when it comes to developing our art. The more we absorb, the more our sense of wonderment. This comes from both watching and riding and not always from the same horses. When both theory and practice are employed in complementary fashion, we can benefit from which each has to offer. What we read in books has limited meaning until we can unearth it for ourselves. Then, as one bright gem of understanding gives way to another – even more translucent – we can return to our books and validate it. That *is* exciting.

And so the questing rider continues on the journey. They know there are many more discoveries still to be made but, being patient, realise they will come to the light in their own time. This requires an open mind, patience, feel, imagination and listening to the horse. Once an insight is understood and confirmed through practice, they may then go on to use it with all their horses, remembering to apologise to the older ones for the fact it has taken so long.

Clearly, the more we improve ourselves, the more we will naturally discover that there are more questions than answers. One vital point of understanding only opens our eyes to the next. A good horseman or horsewoman knows there is always more to learn and it is true that every horse brings another dimension to our riding. Complacency only blurs the need for self-improvement.

For those who are serious in their quest, turning to the work of past or more modern Masters of Equitation can be inspiring. Even if their wise words only confirm what we already know, the validation of our studies is uplifting. It is comforting to know we are all travellers on the same path.

For those who argue things have changed and that only 'modern' techniques should be studied, one is tempted to ask if the wheel has been reinvented. It would be rare indeed that something that is done today hasn't been tried before. Besides, the horse has not changed very much since humankind first took to the saddle, so it is ridiculous to suggest that the classical works are irrelevant. Although there may be some anomalies, the classics are immensely

Try not to think of sitting down hard into your horse. Rather, think of him rising up to meet you.

practical as well as refreshingly clear. Some ancient authors go into far greater depth than most modern writers could possibly hope to achieve.

For me, it is often the cavalry books that clarify a particular point. We are talking of a method developed long before horses were galloped mindlessly in a mass charge towards the guns – as in the film *War Horse*. Instead, light cavalry was made up of highly skilled independent units – horse and man together, fighting hand to hand, face to face. Often, horse and man would share the same humble sod, their only pillow at night. The riders lived and breathed horses. It is humbling to realise that today's dressage movements all stem from exercises being taught at that time. The object was to school the horse to be light on the bridle and easily managed – not so much for show, but for competence, ease and survival.

Without teaching the horse to bring his weight back, the rider had no hope of instant control – he needed the forehand raised, light and manageable. The means to advance, retreat, turn on the spot, leap and move sideways – often in the thick of a mêlée – required lightning swift reactions. With the reins held in one hand, the weapon in the other, flexibility was all. Today we see the same sort of riding still conducted in the Portuguese or Spanish bullring.

The beauty of this training was/is its practicality. Every rider depended upon his horse for his life and the horse seemed to know that the same went for him. Thus there developed an immense sense of partnership, where the horse would not hesitate to sidestep and pick up his rider if balance was lost. The same can be achieved in dressage today but it is not always the case. Many horses clearly love their riders, but there are just as many who have no feelings left in them at all.

When it comes to the higher level work, the rule is simple. Whatever the movement, we must first prepare by bringing the weight back. Only then do we have somewhere to spring from.

Whereas competition used to be judged with those same aspirations of lightness and dexterity, times have changed. Rule No. 1 in the FEI Object and General Principles may still be enshrined in the handbook, but while it was taken seriously until the early post-war era, there are judges today who, consciously or not, appear to disregard it. As Podhajsky suggests in *The Art of Dressage*, modern judging criteria can swing like a pendulum – 'the decisions of the different judges often pointing in opposite directions, making it impossible for the rider to gain any useful advice'. This cannot help anyone, let alone the horse.

The biomechanics of piaffe is weight in the quarters, lightness of the forehand and elevation of the forelegs. It is sad that some judges today are rewarding the absolute opposite – a travesty of self-carriage.

Good piaffe

Bad piaffe

Although we saw a refreshing change of emphasis at London's 2012 Olympics, where harmony took precedence over technicality between the final medallists, the criteria still seems to be governed by the mechanics of locomotion. With judges more impressed by athletic strength and an almost robotic rhythm – however achieve – other important aspects such as flexibility and lightness can be overlooked. Certain winning riders give the appearance that they achieve the requirements of the test *despite* the horse's superior power rather than *because* of it. This is a very different approach from the vision of a horse entrusting his energy to the rider so that the whole picture looks effortless.

I believe it is either fear of the horse's great strength or this idea of rider domination that has caused the proliferation of gadgets and 'training' devices which have become part and parcel of today's training yards. If riders are no longer taught the classical aids to achieve control; if they cannot distinguish between a light seat and a heavy one, a light contact or a strong one, a light horse or a heavy one – then nothing will change. It would be tragic indeed for the horse if lightness were no longer sought in the very place where it should reign supreme.

With the focus out of kilter, many trainers seem more concerned with teaching the rider to control the front end of the horse, rather than developing the weight-bearing capability behind the saddle. As for the requirement to 'support' the horse with the rein, there is nothing wrong with a quiet, steady, even contact, but when we hear that the horse cannot be engaged unless we have so many pounds of weight in our hands, this is neither scientific, pertinent to the classical ideal, or truthful.

So who is really comfortable with this state of affairs? Certainly not the horse, whose natural exuberance and generosity should be a thing of wonder. And can riders really want to feel that every ride must end in a struggle? Surely it is time for a sea-change to get back to basics in *all the disciplines* – to teach the correct aids that the cavalry developed so succinctly in order, effectively, to put the cart right back behind the horse again?

With educated aiding, the rider is now in a position to go one step further. With his weight back, the horse can be fine-tuned in the way of the Masters to show a softer, more elastic way of going. The *descente de main* has always been used as a proof of good balance, and is the final touch to the total acceptance of the bridle. This is a very different concept from using the contact as a balancing tool – rather, it encourages the horse to offer self-carriage. Sustained for more than a few seconds at a time, it is also a wonderful proof.

Even in the soft passage, the forelegs should still be higher than the hindlegs and the neck must arch forward in an unbroken line.

The future of dressage lies in the judging criteria. Until trainers and judges can be instructed to recognise the difference between a horse on the forehand and a horse in self-carriage, contention will grow. What rider who prefers their horses to be light in the hand, will want to be judged in the public arena where the horse who is trying to burst through his reins is preferred? Or, when the horse whose head slants back into his slavered chest gets a higher mark than the relaxed one who can see where he is going? For those with high ideals, it must take real courage to go out there and compete today.

For the future, it will take some serious self-examination and imaginative forward planning amongst the governing bodies of the disciplines to eradicate stress and promote better riding practices in the arenas of the world. Yet improvements can be made and those riders of quality, who presented their horses with such élan and empathy at the London Olympics have made a great start. Their skills should now be encouraged in every country and at every level. Training should focus on the ethos and precepts of classical riding and these must be allowed to filter down to the lower levels and particularly the riding schools.

Until this happens, the great divide will continue. Some competitive practitioners will sneer at the classical adherents, and the classical school will rail against certain elements of competition. When the ideal of what we should be looking for in a simple dressage test is so divided, disharmony will hang over the sport like a black cloud. This is such a pity; it does no good for riders, let alone our kind, generous, willing horses.

Without this horse, I wouldn't have written this book. Thank you Prazer for all your sense of fun, generosity and wisdom.

All this is very sad for the discipline and it is worse when even the so-called 'classical' people disagree. Too many jump onto bandwagons with ignorant self-righteousness which does far more harm than good and the saying 'a little knowledge is dangerous' is only too true. What is needed more than anything is good theory as well as practice and, only by working together to make this available to all, will life for the riding horse improve.

So for now, all one can attempt to do is not be afraid to speak the truth. We must abandon all harshness in riding, reject the 'quick-fix' brigade and educate, educate, educate. There should be no secrecy but an atmosphere of openness throughout. At competitions, no matter how grand, the public should be welcomed to view general exercise and warm-up areas. 'Closed doors' must open! No self-respecting training centre should be afraid to show their horses both in their stable and in the school. The sport must become transparent so we can demonstrate by example how the horse should be ridden and, more importantly, how he would like to be ridden. This should demonstrate – equally importantly – how he does not.

We should never be afraid to ask questions; we do so of our horses, so why not of ourselves? Once the truth is out we will be halfway there. Perhaps not in my lifetime, but who knows? Of one thing, you can be sure of … the horses will be waiting. They look to every one of you for their future.

CLASSICAL QUOTES

'When a horse does not obey the aids, one should not curse him. It is the rider who should apologise, because it is nearly always his own fault.'

— BURGER, GERMAN SCHOOL

✦

'The application of invisible and inaudible aids is one of the principles of classical horsemanship.'

— PODHAJSKY, SCHOOL OF VIENNA

✦

'If we riders do not have absolute control over every part of our body, how can we hope to be able to communicate our wishes to the horse?'

— KOTTAS, SCHOOL OF VIENNA

✦

'The Aids are various, and are to be given in different manners, upon different occasions, they are only meant to accompany the ease and smoothness of the Horse in his air, and to form and maintain the justness of it all.'

— BOURGELAT, FRENCH SCHOOL

✦

'A horse will never tire of a rider who possesses both tact and sensitivity because he will never be pushed beyond his possibilities.'

— OLIVEIRA, PORTUGUESE SCHOOL

✦

'Release of the aids means that the aids should quit as soon as they have acknowledged a response. They bring about, restore, transform, they never maintain.'

— RACINET, FRENCH SCHOOL

'Even the smallest progress is worthy of being praised and celebrated.'

— HEUSCHMANN, GERMAN SCHOOL

✦

'Stirrup weighing is an aid that can be used with horses as perfectly balanced as High-School horses must be, but they are dancers.'

— BURGER, GERMAN SCHOOL

✦

'This liberty [of the reins] gives such confidence to the horse that he unconsciously yields himself to his rider, and becomes his slave whilst thinking that he preserves his absolute independence.'

— BAUCHER, FRENCH SCHOOL

✦

'Lightness in the hand is the base of all true movement.'

— BLAQUE BELLAIR, SCHOOL OF SAUMUR

✦

'The shaping and honing of the horse's natural beauty and energies, in the custody of an inspired equestrian, will not only preserve what Nature bequeathed to the horse, but glorify it in splendour.'

— DE KUNFFY, HUNGARIAN SCHOOL

THOUGHTS FOR THE
FUTURE

T HE FEI (Fédération Equestre Internationale) was officially con-
vened in May 1921 in Paris to lay down a set of rules and a code of practice
for the future of dressage in international competition. In 1930, the following
statement was published:

*'The FEI instituted an International Dressage Event in 1929 in order to protect the
Equestrian Art from the abuses to which it can be exposed and to preserve it in purity
of its principles, so that it could be handed on intact to generations of riders to come.'*
From that standard emanated today's Object and General Principles which
was incorporated into the Rules for each national federation and is still in use
today at the Olympics and in all affiliated competitions.

There is real concern in the world today that a number of horses, seen to
be winning and rewarded in competition up to the highest FEI level, have not
been schooled ethically. By that I mean, there is evidence that horses' heads
have been forced into an unnatural position – which bears no relation to self-
carriage – and that this practice is not just confined to one country or another
but is widespread. Horror stories about horses having their heads fixed into
place in the stable and left to stand, often for hours at a time, to 'develop' the
right muscles and to 'learn' flexion abound. There are enough reliable wit-
nesses to give credence to the rumours, which does equestrian sport no good.

Some riders are seen to school their horses quite openly with the head and
neck forcibly lowered either by an unremitting contact, a severe bit or a gadget
designed for the same purpose. Brave, powerful showjumpers are asked to
take off virtually blind while too many dressage horses are forced to look at

their own forefeet except in those exercises, e.g. canter pirouette, where the movement simply could not take place without the necessary raising of head and forehand. Although warm-up dressage arenas are now monitored for the more extreme forms of abuse, is this enough?

The crux of the matter lies in the fact that there seems little incentive in the entire system to encourage lightness. Riders are rarely taught to develop a seat that promotes light hands unless they go to a specialist. Trainers focus on the horse and often fail to correct the rider. Judges are not helped to reward empathetic equitation since there is only one overall mark for riding *per se* but, as this is generally an average of the rest of the test, it serves little purpose. Luckily, there are still some judges who stick their necks out!

Certain schools and colleges seem particularly at fault. 'Outline' is the buzz word, with contact measured in terms of weight and a sense of entitlement, long before students have even learned to sit. As for learning the leg aids, apart from 'kick!' this is often bypassed. What is encouraged by some is to pull the horse into 'a shape'. Yet, if those instructors stopped to think, they might recognise that it takes sensitivity and skill to ride a horse correctly 'on the bit' – a term which, of itself, is much misunderstood.

Reverse the clock and we read that, in the early 1970s, Colonel Podhajsky, late Director of the Spanish Riding School, was complaining of a culture of 'erroneous' judgments. With the experience of at least two Olympic Games, both as a competitor and later as a judge behind him, his expressed desire was 'to establish or restore the authority and superiority of the dressage judge'. This, he added, 'could only be gained and preserved by absolute impartiality and perfect command of the subject'.

There is no doubt that Podhajsky would abhor the preoccupation with 'outline' which has now pervaded the dressage world. But it is not too late to bring about a sea-change. If the FEI has the purity of the art at heart, rather than the entertaining of spectators, the balance could still be tipped in favour of the horse. It is ridiculous that classical dressage is now seen as something apart from competition dressage. The two should be one and the same.

There are still some highly talented competitors out there who pursue the classical principles as best they can and we saw a fair number riding correctly and even going on to win at the 2012 London Olympics. This shows that the wind of change is blowing. Nevertheless, it cannot be easy for them when there is still a fashion to shorten the horse's neck and ride overbent – and it would require some courage in the judging huts too!

Admittedly, a horse may seem to move more extravagantly when he is held in, and I know myself that if one over-shortens the rein in, say, extended trot, the horse will throw out his forelegs more dramatically than if he is allowed to flow and lengthen throughout his body. For me, one is staccato and the other is natural, but for the sake of the horse we must better educate the public to recognise the difference. A serious rider should never be tempted down that route – even if the ignorant do chant 'Wow!'

As for teachers and trainers, without some knowledge of biomechanics, it will be very hard to bring about change. It is an unfortunate truth of human nature that people want rapid results and if this not discouraged from within the education system itself, shortcuts will inevitably creep in. Until there is a noticeable discrepancy in the competition results between those who ride with invisible aids and the heavy-handed, nothing will change. If this means changing an ethos which is currently so prevalent, so be it.

Dressage is crying out for a system where judges can recognise and are prepared to discriminate between what is good for the horse and what is not. An unnatural posture of the head and neck should be openly shunned; the correct, passively raised neck of a horse moving in self-carriage with superior engagement must be rewarded. With more judges taking a lead to preserve standards, trainers would also be encouraged to follow the letter and the spirit of the FEI Rules and pass it on to their students.

Improvements must start at the bottom of the tree. An honest trainer will explain to their students that horses are not machines. They should be able to reassure their pupils that judges at Preliminary and Novice level will not mark down horses who are not yet fully on the bit. They should explain that it takes time to achieve balance and collection and this is definitely not expected until a higher stage. To be credible, however, they will need the backing and the courage of the judges.

Judges, trainers and riders alike must be made aware that arriving at 'roundness' can only be done by degrees and the process starts in the hind end. The natural process whereby the horse's head 'hangs' from the atlas joint no longer happens automatically once a load is placed on his back. To flex correctly, the horse must learn to engage his hind legs and back muscles and rebalance to compensate for the restrictions placed upon him. As we have seen throughout the preceding chapters, this is not done in a day. It depends on many exercises, quietly and progressively introduced. Again, the dressage tests were originally designed to help this process.

Given the fact that few horses are custom-made precision machines, just what is perfect balance? Picture a horse who carries himself proudly – with well-engaged hocks, well-matched action of both hind and forelegs, loose shoulders, roundness of silhouette emanating from behind and passing over a soft, supple back to end in a high arched neck, with the poll the highest point. From this point the head should flex naturally towards the perpendicular, with the muzzle just in front of or just on the vertical and a relaxed jaw. That is the end to which we should all aspire, but it must not be expected at the beginning!

Of course none of us is perfect and I sometimes cringe at the thought of things I may have done, or inadvertently not done, to improve life for my horses along the way. When I rode competitively, I believe I schooled for far too long at a time without a break, but now I know better. Unfortunately, it is of no comfort at all when I see even the best trainer in the world giving a clinic and forgetting to order a break. That quality down-time is rarely wasted and I see many horses crying out for it. As Paillard, the famous French cavalry instructor always said, if only horses could whine or yelp like dogs, dressage would change overnight.

To protect the horse, we need patience, empathy, feel and *understanding* for every action he takes and every move he makes. If truth be known, being in tune with the animal underneath you is as intimate and vital as being in bed with your lover ... and since this is the truth, I am not blushing. It is also true to say we generally expect far less physically of our human partners than we do of our horses, so it is not surprising when some horses object.

Impure, erratic or irregular gaits rarely emanate spontaneously from the horse unless there is some form of pain or unsoundness. More generally, they are the result of rider interference or something quite simple, like an over-tight noseband or curb. We can all make mistakes, but as long as these are not prolonged or habitual, the horse is generally very forgiving.

Never be afraid to seek help but, whatever you do, choose an educated trainer. Such a person will look at you and the horse together, may ride him themselves and, if the problems are insurmountable, will go back to basics. This may mean lungeing and loose-schooling but at least any physical problem will then, generally, come to light. If none is found, the trainer will then set about improving the rider, which will inevitably lead to improving the horse.

Let us therefore take a step back and base our work on classical precepts and Nature's own laws. A leaf could be taken out of the example set by the Spanish Riding School which, incidentally, draws more spectators than competition dressage has ever achieved (the Olympics excepted). In Vienna, it has long been recognised that it takes at least eight years or more to complete a horse's training. Why should that knowledge not encourage and inspire today? To take a horse from scratch and work up the levels is an amazing, stimulating and thrilling process. The prize – a wonderful sense of ease, spontaneity and grace in each and every movement, without any apparent effort. Clearly, disciplining ourselves as much as the horse underneath us brings huge and lasting fulfilment.

Competition should, therefore, help you along the way and should not be disdained. Properly conducted, it should be enjoyable and fun for horses and riders and provide a yardstick for progress. Remember, however, that judging is totally subjective and under the present system your results are not necessarily a benchmark of your ability. Every horse is different and breed preferences may influence the final result. So do not be depressed if you and the judge beg to differ – be ruled by the progress of your horse. Ultimately, it would be refreshing to see a mixture of breed and type performing at the higher levels, which in itself would draw more support from the public. Robot-like performances with horse after horse 'cast in the same mould' do not necessarily draw the crowds. Variety is, after all, the spice of life.

For now, the main thing is to enjoy your horse. Do not get too hung up on the opinions of others, and always, *always* end your work on a good note. Remember – Nature knows best and if your horse grows in beauty as a result of your partnership, that should be reward enough. It should fill us with wonder, that this of all the animals is the only one that allows us to share and hopefully preserve his perfect balance. That in itself is an inspiration to study and ride better. I hope this book will have helped you and your horses along your chosen path.

SCHOOL EXERCISES

Chapter by Chapter

THESE SCHOOL EXERCISES are not intended to replace hacking, jumping, gridwork or trotting poles, which are all important parts of the education of all horses in conjunction with the work of the manège. They are given below in a progressive order, applicable to the chapter in question (but not necessary to the level of training).

Some stages may take years to hone and refine. Clearly, every horse is different and only the rider can judge whether or not the horse is sufficiently mature, willing or comfortable to advance his education through the different stages. Always start each new exercise in walk and do not progress to trot or canter (where appropriate) until it is understood and the horse is at ease in the work. Throughout each and every phase of schooling always start and finish on a long rein, with plenty of stretches in between.

CHAPTER 2

- Ride large and out to the track in walk, trot (and canter with mature horse) with frequent changes of rein across the diagonal.

- Use short diagonals, e.g. B-H as well as long ones e.g. F-H (walk/trot).

- Ride half figures of eight, e.g. back to back half-circles (walk/trot).

- Use turns down the centre line – but not for 'baby' horses – to assess balance (walk/trot).

- Support the horse with inside leg at girth (toe roughly opposite girth) every time you approach the track or ride a corner. Open the outside rein to help.

- On straight lines and turns, keep hips and shoulders aligned with the horse.

- Make frequent upward and downward progressive transitions – thinking up! – for both.

- Halt in different places from time to time (legs just behind girth) – count to six – give the rein and move on

- Always end with something easy – i.e. on a good note.

CHAPTER 3

In addition to the exercises suggested in Chapter 2:

- Ride 20m circles equally on both reins in between your straight work (walk/trot).

- Ride half a 20m circle in trot and half in canter. Gradually increase the canter strides until you ride a full 20m circle – then ride straight up the track.

- Ride zigzags, e.g. K-B-H on both reins (walk/trot).

- Introduce full figures of eight, riding straight through the centre (walk/trot).

- Ride a 15m half-circle near the end of the track and return to the wall on a long diagonal, changing the inside flexion (just a shade) well before you arrive on the track (walk/trot).

- Ride large round part of the school – e.g. in a 20 x 40m school, pretend it's shrunk to 20 x 30m.

- At least once in every schooling session, halt, pause, rein back two or three steps (only one step initially, if you have never done this before) and immediately return to walk, followed by stretch on a long rein.

CHAPTER 4

In addition to exercises suggested in Chapters 2 and 3:

- Ride deeper into the corners, with your inside leg at the girth and an open outside rein.

- Move off the long sides towards the quarter lines making a shallow loop of 3m with soft inside bend when both leaving the track and in the return (walk/trot/canter)

- Ride half figures of eight in canter with a transition to trot through the centre.

- Introduce serpentines of three loops on both reins – each loop to touch the track (walk/trot) Straighten for at least five strides through middle of each loop before preparing for new bend

- From a quarter marker, e.g. H on the right rein, ride a 10m half-circle and return to the track (in this example just before K) on a diagonal line (walk/trot).

- Improve your circles in canter – thinking soft inside rein; inside leg like a pillar.

- On a 15m circle in walk, ride half the circle normally – half in shoulder-fore. Keep your inside hip slightly in advance of the outside one for a normal circle; at the halfway point, turn both hips and shoulders to look to the inside for shoulder-fore.

CHAPTER 5

In addition to exercises suggested in Chapters 2, 3 and 4:

- Ride figures of eight as two 15m circles with only two or three strides straight through the centre (in trot).

- Ride a 15m circle and gradually spiral down to 10m (walk/trot). Weight to the inside, retain soft inside flexion – but move the outside rein against the horse's neck to guide the forehand inward.

- Spiral a 10m circle outward until it becomes 15m (walk/trot). Use more pressure from your inside leg at the girth to move out – the inside rein moving against the horse's neck, opening the outside rein, and more weight on your outside stirrup. *NB both spiralling exercises must be progressive*

- Ride 10m half-circles off the track (in trot) and return to the track with your outside rein alone.

- Ride large squares in the centre of the school – thinking more outside rein than inside (walk/trot),

- Ride 15m circles in canter, then spiral out (think inside leg to outside rein) and continue down the track.

- Ride a 10m circle followed by two or three steps in shoulder-in (walk) up the track, then move immediately onto a diagonal with support of your outside rein to confirm the angle, and change the rein. Repeat the exercise on new track, new rein.

CHAPTER 6

In addition to exercises suggested in Chapters 2, 3, 4 and 5:

- Continue spiralling exercises, being more aware of your outside leg (and outside rein) as you spiral down (in trot).

- Canter 20m circles and spiral down to 15m (thinking outside leg and outside rein).

- Ride a 10m circle (walk/later trot) followed by four or five steps of shoulder-in on the track with your outside knee and thigh in support, then straighten on the long side, having relaxed your outside leg.

- Ride normal 15m circles (in walk/later trot), with two or three steps only of quarters-in for part of circle. For the latter, turn your hips and shoulders to the outside, deepen your inside knee and weight your inside stirrup. Ask the horse to step sideways away from outside leg pressure to bend around your inside leg.

- Improve canter work with transitions: downward to trot; upward from walk. Make clear contrasts between both leg aids. Deepen your weight into the inside stirrup in the strike-off – lighten your outside seat bone and 'open' your outside hip joint to clarify the 'ask' aid from your outside leg behind the girth.

- Vary the size of loops in walk, trot and canter.

- Ride 90-degree turns on the hocks (quarter pirouette) – *in walk* – at E or B, then straighten to X with soft inside flexion, weight to the inside, outside rein against horse's neck.

CHAPTER 7

Building on work from preceding chapters:

- Improve and refine all transitions generally.

- Ride circles and serpentines making transitions within each gait. Think 'bigger strides' or 'more collected' in all you do.

- Rely less on your hands and use your upper body and core in both upward and downward transitions. Feel how your seat bones move forward as you draw up.

- Introduce simple changes and half-halts in canter, to rebalance on corners, turns or transitions.

- Introduce travers from a 10m circle on the long sides (walk/later trot) always straightening after four or five good steps.

- Ride shoulder-in and shoulder-fore in trot.

- Ride 15m half-circles in canter, returning to the track on a diagonal line, and continue in counter-canter. Gradually think more sideways (use outside rein indirectly) on the diagonal, with a feel for half-pass.

- Spiral circles up or down in canter.

- Ride rein-back to canter for more collection.

- In all exercises, sit tall with your seat as close to the pommel as is comfortable.

CHAPTER 8

Building on work from preceding chapters:

- Ride a 20m circle with 4 x 10m circles at each 'quarter marker' of the circle on both reins (in trot).

- Gradually join these up (using your inside rein indirectly) in shoulder-fore (trot).

- Later, ride half the exercise in shoulder-fore; half in travers.

- Improve shoulder-in on the track (inside rein used indirectly) and allow your outside rein to support or open according to the angle/balance of your horse.

- From a 10m circle, ride travers (in trot) on the track with normal aids and outside rein used indirectly.

- From a 10m circle in a corner of arena, start two or three steps of half-pass on a diagonal line (in walk/later trot) – same aids as for travers – then go forward straight for a few strides; then half-pass again. Build on this gradually until you can go sideways and forwards across the school on the same rein to the other side with ease.

- Once your horse is confident to offer more lateral steps, ride the same exercise to the centre line, straighten for two strides, and change the bend (and rein) to progress in the same fashion from X back to the track. Never hesitate to go straight forward again if you lose impulsion, bend, rhythm or angle.

- Refine the canter half-pass with more collection and bend. *(NB: canter half-pass involves no crossing; the horse moves sideways in a series of bounds within the canter gait, whereas half-pass in walk and trot require, if anything, more tact, timing and separation between the direct and indirect aids.)*

CHAPTER 9

Building on work from preceding chapters:

- Improve collection with lateral work on the centre line or quarter line –say six steps shoulder-in, six steps travers, with 10m circles in between.

- Ride zigzags in half pass – first in walk, then in trot – always straighten between each change of rein.

- Ride 15m circles half in collected walk, half in extended walk.

- Ride 20m circles, half in collected trot, half in medium trot.

- Ride 20m circles, half in collected canter, half in medium canter.

- Ride 10m circle (collected trot) at F or K, H or M – change the rein to X, continue in medium trot – collect again on the opposite track.

- Ride 10m circles in the corner in collected gaits, then extend up the track and later

- on diagonals.

- Alternate between collected and medium gaits on straight lines.

- Use corners with a few steps of lateral work prior to all lengthening, medium and extended work.

- Ride counter-canter on 20m circles – excellent for stretching the loins.

- Ride canter half-pass to X, then straighten into medium canter up the centre line.

- Introduce a feel for canter shoulder-in on corners prior to extending up the long side.

CHAPTER 10

Building on work from preceding chapters:

- Keep the work enterprising, entertaining and diligent as you warm up. Use all the lateral exercises in short spells to flex joints, supple and soften, and concentrate the horse's mind before starting the changes.

- Ride shoulder-out (looking at the track) and renvers (looking into the school).

- Refine all transitions.

- Canter to walk; walk to canter should now be fully established.

- Rein-back to canter should be fluid and calm.

- Simple changes should involve fewer and fewer steps until the one step in between is replaced by a flying change.

- Other exercises which may invite a spontaneous change include:

  – Circle in counter-canter with change at the furthest 'point'.

  – Figure or half-figure of eight – with a change in the centre.

  – Diagonal line with more collection prior to change at X.

  – Half-pass back to the track with a change on arrival.

  – Later, zigzags in canter half-pass with change of leg as appropriate.

- In all cases, always straighten the horse prior to asking for a change then soften the new inside rein into which he has to flex. Gradually this will present an invitation to him to *want* to change.

CHAPTER 11

Building on work from preceding chapters:

- The warm-up should now comprise a *mélange* of all the movements practised to date.

- In between all the exercises, hone, harmonise and try to reduce the aids for each request. At this stage, subtlety is all, and 'little and often' is good. For example:

- Five steps of shoulder-in, into five steps of half-pass, into five steps straight, followed by a demi-pirouette, following by four steps of travers up the quarter-line, followed by four steps of shoulder-in ... followed by walk on a long rein.

- Without collection, there can be no happy transition into the piaffe, passage or canter pirouette. These movements can, I am told, be taught by rapping horses on the leg, beating their rumps, even attaching pulleys to their fetlocks ...yet a fit, happy horse will offer them naturally and with great pride.

- Every exercise which increases the flexion of the hind limb joints and therefore the ability of the horse to collect will be appropriate for these movements. A happy horse is like a well-oiled machine, moving effortlessly through every gait, transition, every change of gear – the whole thing should be seamless.

I will not insult the reader by prescribing each and every movement in a special order at this point. If one cannot feel what needs to be done, one should perhaps refrain from requesting the movements described in this chapter and put them off to another day.

CHAPTER 12

You do not have to be an advanced rider to do this one-handed work. Provided you use your seat, upper body and leg aids correctly, one-handed riding should pose little problem to the well-educated rider. It can be started halfway through the horse's career (although the full spectrum of movements is included below).

- Only commence the one-handed work when the horse feels soft, supple and mentally relaxed. Start simply and progressively and take time on the following:

Straight lines and big circles.

Serpentines and loops.

Turns on the hocks.

Upward and downward transitions.

Rein-back.

Transitions within the gait.

Lateral work on the circle.

Lateral work on the track.

Counter-canter.

Flying changes

Piaffe, passage and pirouette.

As with everything, proceed step by patient step and, to begin, do only a little at a time … then give the rein … and reward.

REFERENCES

Albrecht, Brigadier General Kurt, *A Dressage Judge's Handbook*, J.A. Allen, 1988

Astley, Philip, *Astley's Equestrian Education*, Tibson, 1801

Baucher, François, *The Principles of Horsemanship*, Vinton & Co, 1919

Beudant, Etienne, *Exterieure et Haute Ecole*, Amat, 1923

Blignault, Karin, *Equine Biomechanics for Riders*, J.A. Allen, 2009

Blacque Belair, *Cavalry Horsemanship and Horse Training*, Vinton & Co Ltd, 1918

Blixen-Finecke, Lt Col Hans Von, *The Art of Riding*, J.A. Allen, 1977

Bourgelet, Claude, *A New System of Horsemanship*, Paul Vaillant, 1754

Burger, Üdo, *The Way to Perfect Horsemanship*, J.A. Allen, 1986

Decarpentry, General Albert, *Academic Equitation*, J.A. Allen, 1971

Faverot de Kerbrecht, Baron F de, *Dressage Methodique du Cheval de Selle*, Paris, 1891

Fillis, James, *Breaking and Riding,* 1902 (reprint J.A. Allen, 1969)

Froissard, Jean, *Classical Horsemanship for Our Time*, Cox and Wyman, 1971

Guérinière, François Robichon Sieur de la, *Ecole de Cavalerie,* Paris, 1733

Hester, Carl and Faurie, Bernadette, *Down to Earth Dressage*, Kenilworth Press, 1999

Heuschmann, Dr Gerd, *Tug of War – Classical Versus "Modern" Dressage,*
  J.A. Allen, 2007

Balancing Act, J.A. Allen, 2012

Jousseaume, Col Andre, *Progressive Dressage*, J.A. Allen, 1978

Klimke, Dr Reiner, *Basic Training of the Young Horse*, J.A. Allen, 1985

Kottas-Heldenberg, Arthur, *Kottas on Dressage*, Kenilworth Press, 2010

Kunffy, Charles de, *The Ethics and Passions of Dressage*, Half Halt Press, 1993

Liçart, Comm. Jean, *Basic Equitation*, J.A. Allen, 1968

Müseler, Wilhelm, *Riding Logic*, Eyre Methuen, 1965

Newcastle, William Cavendish, Duke of, *A General System of Horsemanship*,
  Antwerp, 1743

Oliveira, Nuno, *Reflections on Equestrian Art*, J.A. Allen, 1976

Classical Principles of theArt of Training Horses, Howley & Russell, 1983

From an Old Master Trainer To Young Trainers, Howley & Russell, 1986

Paillard, Col Jean Saint-Fort, *Understanding Equitation*, Doubleday & Co, 1974

Pembroke, Henry Herbert, 10th Earl of, *Military Equitation*, 1778

Peters, Lt Col J.G., *The Art of Horsemanship*, Whittaker & Co, 1835

Podhajsky, Col Alois, *The Complete Training of Horse and Rider*, Harrap,
  London, 1967

The Art of Dressage, Harrap, London 1979

Basic Principles of Riding and Judging, Harrap, 1976

Print, Patrick, *The BHS Complete Manual of Horsemanship*, Kenilworth, 2011

Racinet, Jean-Claude, *Racinet explains Baucher*, Xenophon, 1997

Seunig, Waldemar, *Horsemanship*, Doubleday & Co 1974

Van Schaik, Dr H.L.M., *Misconceptions and Simple Truths in Dressage,*
  J.A. Allen, 1986

Wynmalen, Henry, *Equitation*, Country Life Publications, 1946

Dressage – A Study of the Finer Points of Riding, Museum Press, 1953

The Horse in Action, Harold Starke Ltd, 1964

INDEX